God Bless America

God Bless America

Absurdities In American Life

by Allen L. Scarbrough

Writers Club Press
San Jose New York Lincoln Shanghai

God Bless America
Absurdities In American Life

Writers Club Press
an imprint of iUniverse, Inc.

For information address:
iUniverse, Inc.
5220 S. 16th St., Suite 200
Lincoln, NE 68512
www.iuniverse.com

Opinions expressed are the authors only.

ISBN: 0-595-22068-1

Printed in the United States of America

To my wife Debra.

Perfect laws can only be made by perfect men, to the end of time, we will never see either one.

Contents

Introduction

I t is hard to know where to begin this voyage of exploration. America is a country as vast and varied as any on earth. From pilgrims to the present day Americans have possessed a spirit of ingenuity and resolve that is the envy of the world. Yet, tucked into the fabric of our prosperous society is an undercurrent of recklessness and misunderstanding. We Americans are too busy to examine our lives. I'm not busy at all, so I've taken it upon myself to penetrate the stratums of our society and report our coming and goings for you. I hope you agree the expedition is worth the risk that you might perceive yourself in a fresh, and possibly unfavorable, light. But you might just find that as Americans we are a brazen, yet likeable bunch.

America was founded on principles drafted by genius, and like all such endeavors, the labors of the highest faculties of the human mind are ultimately bestowed upon the mediocre. Thus our absurd society as it is today. I entice you along this maze of madness that you might grasp the role you play in life, though I must warn you, that role might not be as exciting as you have imagined. Americans are the lovers of all things practical, but freedom is quite impractical. Freedom is a burden for which payment must be extorted and that payment is an inspection of our beliefs, pursuits and ideas. Let us start with a brief history lesson.

The Founding Fathers

✦

(Or strange offspring)

It has been my dream to discover a use for my political science degree. I was advised sixteen years ago that politics was an unfashionable profession. I quarreled long and hard, but alas, I must admit that my fellow students were right. They now manage law practices, dental chairs, corporations and pharmacies. I sell stuff to maintain a roof over my head and that roof leaked a lot last year. At any rate, I will now for the first time in my life (except for the recent interpretations of the Electoral College I was obliged to clarify to my friends) put to use my restricted, yet superficial, knowledge of the founding of our country and discourse on the intellectual capital vital to founding a free country. Of course the first thing that must occur is the country must be founded while the intelligent are still engrossed enough to participate, once the grand fun of swapping verbal blows has dissipated the bright and clever start to travel a lot. In the 1700's you could still get up a rousing game of whack the King and it was so engaging that everybody was doing it.

The founding fathers, an astonishing bunch if you realize the population of America in 1776 was slightly more than four million souls, were like most men through the ages that have bred revolution, except for one endearing fact, most of them were wealthy. The poor start most revolutions, so America was special in this regard. The truth behind the revolution was this-a lot of men were getting stinking rich and didn't want some tyrant thousands of miles overseas to grab any of it. So they

3

rebelled. The rebellion was shrewdly disguised as a moral crusade, but make no mistake, the rich longed to get richer.

Now in reality all of the founding fathers should have been beheaded after the English quickly dispensed with the tattered troops of Washington and others, but the English made one fatal error, they lost the bloody war. The victory of the colonies is on a par with me, a sluggish, non-jumping white man, annihilating Michael Jordan in a game of one on one. The English had the supreme armies in the world, but the Americans didn't fight fair. They brawled like Indians and rapscallions, hiding in underbrush, under logs and beneath fence rails, and were able to pick the British off in unsuspecting moments. Contrary to popular belief, the colonists had better rifles than the British, like I said the colonists were getting rich. But to make my belabored point more succinctly the chief difference between being a hero and being hung is victory. Victors revise the end of the story to make them appear more brilliant than they were and the colonists were no exception. Do you really believe Washington tossed a dollar across the Potomac? Good grief people.

Speaking of bogus impressions made through rewritten history, Ben Franklin didn't discover electricity, the equations of electricity preceded him by several years, he instead discovered the electrification of lightening, a much less prestigious achievement, but nonetheless hair-raising. America succeeded in the revolution for one good reason and it wasn't because God was on their side, many more British subjects prayed for the destruction of the colonies than there were colonists, but the success of the little country was predicated on one irresistible idea, that rich makes right. The colonists were ruthless in their zeal that by God no Brits were going to come to their country and rob them blind. (Diamonds always produce more zeal than coal, I suppose). So a country was born, America, based on the declaration that all men are created equal; some are just poorer than others, and some lug chains.

After the success of the revolution, the colonists, having defeated the preeminent army on earth, anointed George Washington king, or rather would have if he had permitted it. George turned down the proposal for one reason; it paid less than his day job, which was marrying wealthy widows and their fortunes. But George also, I surmise, was suspicious of the British and the good fortune he had of winning the war despite losing a majority of the battles he generaled. He rightfully feared vengeance and beheading should the British return with a better-led force and recapture the upstart colonies. George was a shrewd man and I've always admired his shear audacity for good luck, but George Washington the king would never have flown after so much blood had been spilled in the cause of freedom. The price of everything, after all, is gauged by the degree of sacrifice requisite to gain it. I applaud George, but now I live in the aftermath of his good graces, living in a country that lives under the guidance of the Constitution, though not one man in a hundred has ever read it.

So after the War of Independence, or it would be better said, the war in which a small number of fortunate folk hurled dice and rolled sevens, thereby saving their necks, the country began in earnest with the office of president, a congress, a few judges and a horde of lesser lights that would in due course triumph over their superiors by construing the constitution in innumerable ways that the writers never imagined. The first president was of course George Washington. It was reasoned, if he could crush the British against incredible odds then surely he could defeat the stupidity of Congress. Unfortunately, the colonists were dead wrong. George eventually retired and said little of importance for the last years of his life. But then he had said little of importance during the previous years of his life; George was after all, more veneer than wood. Except for his teeth.

The colonists were miraculously lucky to have at their disposal Thomas Jefferson to claim the crown of George after a momentary intermission by John Adams. Thomas was a brilliant scholar and scientist, and though he owned slaves he treasured their company so much he permitted one to bear his children. Thomas Jefferson opposed slavery, but of course he did not free his own. Who would scrub the laundry, he reasoned? Nevertheless, Thomas proved a bit besieged by the position so he retired to his estate, Monticello, pretty nice digs for a planter. It should be noted that he authored the Declaration of Independence, a brilliant article of writing, but the version you now read is of course a butchered edition after it had passed through the hands of various political morons. The original document was so inflammatory that it was watered down with scores of Thomas Jefferson's tears as he watched the hacks chop his masterpiece to bits. It will always be true in this world that brilliance must be dimmed to prevent the blinding of the masses, whose greatest wish is to die rich rather than saved.

No discourse on the founding fathers would be all-inclusive without a reference to Ben Franklin. As I stated before he is not the father of electricity, though he was the father of an illegitimate child. Ben's other claim to fame is the creation of the magazine. Ben is regarded as the savior of the waiting room. How else would we pass time waiting to shell out a stack of money to a guy in a white coat who knows little more than we do about the human anatomy? For this act we, as Americans, are eternally indebted. I credit an article in a yachting magazine in my dentist's office with the motivation for this book. I resolved to abhor the rich and write a book extolling the virtues of poverty and clean living, though in reality I really pined for a yacht. Ben Franklin journeyed to France as our ambassador of wit to sway the French to our cause, an alliance that in the end sealed the fate of the British. Ben amused the French so much, they being thunderstruck that an American could chatter beyond the vernacular of farm implements, that they decided to unite in our cause for freedom. But in truth they sought only to destroy the English, the cause of freedom making so much nobler an excuse than simple hatred.

I'd like to wrap up this opening section by mentioning the great declaration of Nathan Hale, "give me liberty or give me death." This I judge to be the rambling of a mad man. Men sacrifice their freedom each and every day to go to work. There is no perfect liberty in this life. There is merely the freedom to choose one's mode of living, but all modes of living are a prison of sorts. Even my impulse to write is itself a prison. What Nathan should have whispered is this, "give me a career with no boss and early retirement or give me heart disease." Doesn't this ring truer? At any rate, I admire the sentiment and believe the tiny state of New Hampshire has the only state motto worthy of the license plate, "live free or die." My dear New Hampsherites, we will all die, free or not, but nice try.

A Star Is Born

❖

(Or I wish I may, I wish I might)

America rapidly established itself as a formidable economic power by exporting the agricultural products of the south and the manufacturing goods of the north. The Bill of Rights, in establishing the freedom to become wealthy, allowed all Americans to cheerfully chase the making of money, and if things didn't work out in their present surroundings they just packed up and moved west to start fresh. This move often left the families just as destitute, but closer to the Pacific Ocean. All seemed too good to be true, and it was.

The British, having perceived the error of their ways, meaning having allowed a collection of ill groomed frontiersmen beat them in battle, soon grasped the enormous wealth to be made in the lush soil, green grazing land and low hills of America. They returned, just as Washington had feared. This time they battled to a draw and in 1812 a kind of political stalemate was instituted whereby the British conceded that the colonies were a tough bunch and better left alone. Better to trade them blind than shoot them, they reasoned. Let the colonies raise the cotton and wear their soil thin. Let the colonies be our producers and we will consume. The British are often reconciled by summations and love to rationalize defeat by considering the benefits of their slighter station.

The land of promise and slavery prospered off and on for several years until a growing disparity between two halves of the country broke the country into factions. In the north, industrialization was the backbone of the economy. In the south, cotton was king. By God, some reasoned, if a man can't be king then something else will be. Tyrants, after all, are a simpler taskmaster than freedom, which demands constant attention.

So it was in the heart of the nineteenth century that the first great crisis of democracy appeared. America was an experiment, a trial of government to determine if any country, so conceived, could long endure, to paraphrase Abe. Apparently not. America splintered in that day of blood and the country that emerged from the civil war wasn't unified until the First World War, when victory again made Americans proud. At last they could overlook the silly squabble that had decimated six million souls and be together. But that didn't last either, Vietnam, in a word. In between the events of the 1850's and 1918 a small amount of American blood was shed in the Civil War, or War Between the States, or War of Northern Aggression, depending on whether your state won or lost. Mine won, so I shall hereby refer to it as the Civil War, though it was at times most untidily uncivil.

The striking thing about the cause of the south was its utter futility. Not just slavery, which alone would have sealed defeat, but the economic reality that the industrial might of the north was so fearsome that it even kept the British out of the war. This is the very definition of tragedy, to assail against impossible odds though your fate is sealed by unalterable events. That is why we refer to the efforts of the South as noble. It's the only way we can justify the slaughter of so many millions, that it was in defeating a noble enemy. Robert E. Lee has been elevated to the status of military god because his sharp shooting country boys could outshoot a bunch of near illiterate factory workers from Jersey. The south was victorious early in the war because it could shoot straighter. There were no real tactics in the Civil War, only aim, shoot, and die.

But because so much blood had been spilled a bigwig had to come along and say a few suitable words to make it all look worthwhile, though in reality it was a colossal waste of humanity, so Abe Lincoln was called upon at Gettysburg to convey a few words of dedication.

His few chosen words were declared sufficient and the bold statement 'Four score and twenty years ago'…now live in infamy, though young people can scarcely count change for a dollar much less four score and anything. I've traveled to Gettysburg and it is a place of true sadness, particularly the graves of the unknowns. Their heads were blown off, or faces, or too much of something and could not be identified. Nowadays we of course have the dog tag, which enables us to identify all victims of their enemies unless they are vaporized in a nuclear holocaust. All shadows pretty much look alike.

Back to Robert E. Lee. If not for the cantankerously efficient Lee the war might not have lasted a year. For reasons best laid at the doorstep of deity, Lee and his hodgepodge army was able to keep at bay the vast army of the Potomac, though that army had superior equipment, numbers and ammunition. But the odd thing about battle is that somebody with an ample brain must be found to marshal these factors to their greatest effect or they come to nothing. The north never really found such a man. Grant was no tactician, leader, or much of anything except painfully able to lose thousands of men a week in a war of attrition. Grant having 100,000 men to Lees 50,000 simply killed 50,000 of his own men until Lee had none, or almost none. Not exactly brilliant, but I bet Grant could count change. Grant went on to a stellar career as a drunk who lived at the White House. Lee became president of a college, though his estate, Arlington, was made into a national cemetery. I believe the thinking at the time was this-lay the dead soldiers at the doorstep of the man who killed them. Apparently, Lincoln didn't possess a stately enough mansion at the time.

Truth be told the Civil War is still being fought. Americans have always possessed hatred for losing and losing the war has never sat well with the aristocratic, yet impoverished south. The civil rights movement of the sixties was itself a rehashing of the Civil War. The south struggled to cling to those Christian values that had fostered their noble society before the war. Unfortunately, blacks opposed the exclusion of their people from the principles of Christ and marched in the streets in protest. Of course, southern society fought back with the sword of justice at their side, which just so happened to bear a resemblance to a fire hose held to effect by one Bull Conner. Bull Conner just happened to be similar to most southern men of the time, convinced that society was best served by separate yet equal facilities (ironically, blacks were the ones that initially sued to get them.) I find this odd since not once did anyone ever offer to switch places with the other "equal" party. Separate but equal has always meant, and shall always mean, less for you, more for me. In other words, I will be your equal so long as you acknowledge my superiority and generosity. So the Civil War evolved into Civil Rights, but it is all one war, one gigantic war, to determine who will eat the high end of the hog, though it is just one lonely hog.

It is fitting and proper that Abraham Lincoln laid down his life in the cause of freedom. I love old Abe, but he was not honest Abe or any other Abe, just Abe, of the same flesh and bone as you or I. Abraham Lincoln found himself in a quandary at the start of his presidency, the country he'd been elected to govern did not exist, or at least only part of it existed, the other half had disseminated into a new country, founded on principles comparable to the one it had broken from except that slaves were not counted as people, more like livestock or chickens. Abe saw the need to reunite the country. I've never deciphered the why of this. Today we would call him a tyrant for such behavior, let all folks govern themselves and live as they wish, we say. But Abe persevered and through his unalterable quest for reunification six million souls perished. They died to save a principle, America. Abraham Lincoln spilled his blood on the ground and the country was once again free.

Of course today we realize that the cause to which he fought so valiantly was foolishness. His saving grace was the abolition of slavery, which is as cruel to the master as to the servant; for wherever there is a man in prison there is another close at hand to guard him. America would be united and strong today even if the country had never gone to war, but there would be about forty or fifty million more of us, the offspring of the war dead. The south could never have sustained a country or slavery. It would soon have been cheaper to employ squatters to do the dirty work. Field hands by the 1860's were as expensive as small farms. In the end the Civil War gave us many names and heroes, but little genuine enduring truth, except the undying principle that when in the way of cannon it is better to wear a helmet than a cap.

I'd love to write more of the Civil War, a cherished subject of mine, but it would in itself produce an entire book. But let it rest on my head that much of our modern absurdity has sprung from the aftermath of that bloody war. The south didn't die, it just went into hibernation, who knows that it will not rise again. Imagine if you will that a foreign invader had penetrated our soil in 1859 and forestalled the war. Robert E. Lee would have commanded the troops and led our nation to great victory. He would have been elected president and been our greatest hero next to Washington. He was the greatest commander of men to ever stroll this continent, but he fought for a losing cause and is therefore only a shadow in our history. Imagine if you will if Lincoln had been forced to accept a stalemate in the war, unable to find a commander to lead his troops to victory, his name would now be pronounced in the same sentences as Millard Fillmore, Hoover, and Coolidge. Greatness is often the byproduct of good fortune. It is better to be lucky than to be born with great gifts, many of the latter have failed to sway fortune with the prize of greatness though they outshadow the figures of history with their towering potential.

Great men, however, do sometimes come to the fore in times of great crisis, but their deeds are less right or wrong than that they result in the outcome desired by the masses. We make heroes out of ordinary men because we must agree that some men are better than others, but I disagree with the sentences of history, all men are great given the correct circumstances. And all countries are great given that they are rich. America is a great country, Mexico is not. They are separated by a mere invisible line that stretches for hundreds of miles across the barren desert, though this line is no more real than the mirage that guides our footsteps to an empty well.

The Civil War tested the principle of freedom to its utmost degree. Freedom, we found, is fragile. It required the blood of millions of souls to free the slaves, whose presence in this country was predicated on the principle that slaves worked cheap. But in the end it required blood, money, and years of precious time to redirect our country's misstep into folly. The price of slavery is incalculable. In the end the plantation owners lost it all, including many of them their lives and their sons lives and all their dreams, hopes, and desires for the future. If this is not a high price I do not know what else could be. It is easy in this world to take a dollar from a man's pocket, but oh so hard to give it back with interest, especially if that interest has been festering for two hundred years. May slavery rest in the avenues of hell and men never again attempt to circumvent the laws of nature that dictate that men are free only if they grant freedom to all. America survived slavery, barely.

War To End All Wars

✦

(Or how big can I lie)

I n case you just dropped off a turnip truck and are unfamiliar with the ways of men let me teach you a principle true in all times and places. Whenever anyone labels something the last of its kind, they are merely talking about the death of their own imagination. Nature has a way of making idiots out of prognosticators and prophets. World War One, or The War To End All Wars as it was pronounced, was so viscous and cruel as to make all future pretenses to war a ghastly and unthinkable event. Today of course we would call the slaughter of early twentieth century Europe tame by comparison to the slaughter in our glorious, futuristic world. But at least they made the attempt to make it the last war by forming the United Nations. However, this vehicle for peace runs about as well as a Yugo. If it is necessary to pronounce a war-The War To End All Wars-in order to get Americans to fight in it, then I imagine the best way to end all wars is to cease showing up for them. But alas, someone has trained you that there are principles worth dying for, mostly these are people who do not fight the wars, but sit in Washington and count the totals of the dead (mostly you and me). I believe there is little worth dying for, even a victorious country is often felled in the future by some subsequent folly. To save your children or wife or your personal freedom is perhaps an exception, but I warn you not to die for a principle, there are no eternal principles in life, there are only some that live longer than others.

America entered the fray in Europe after a prolonged stalemate had turned the whole mess into a trench war of certain death. Mustard gas, senseless frontal assaults and methods of the past gave way to the modern war, a war of outliving your opponent. America entered this ruckus with the enthusiasm of a teenager eager to lose his virginity. We won the war primarily because we didn't understand the realities of trench warfare and killed people instead. The allies eventually overcame the German aggressors and then blundered into the greatest mistake of all history by impoverishing the vanquished foe. The America that emerged from this era was a hardened and bitter country that soon would be forever tempered by the great depression. The War To End All Wars did end something for all time however, the love of war.

America had grown from an infant to a young adult on the isolation afforded it by our separation from the great European powers by two oceans. This prolonged adolescence was the very fire that lit our way into the First World War. We loved our isolation, but we loved adventure more. It is hard to believe that the whole mess started with the assassination of a single man, a man that represented the past and not the future. The Archduke of Austria must have been the most incredible man to have ever lived because his assassination was deemed by mankind to be worth the sacrifice of tens of millions of lives. America sacrificed thousands of young men to the cause, though not more than ten or twenty fully understood the stupidity to which they had been duped to their deaths.

America lusted for the soil of Europe and many of our young men are now planted six feet deep in the sod they so hungered for. But if there is a saving grace to all that was lost it was this, America became a superpower at last and took its rightful station among the giants of the earth. Except for this change America might not have been prepared for Hitler. If not for America, Hitler might have ruled the world. A world ruled by Hitler would have been indistinguishable from hell. So America traipsed across the ocean to fight, and fight they did, until the Germans agreed to an Armistice. An Armistice is where one country no longer wishes to fight the war even though it is winning. Kind of like a tie when the score is uneven. Europe settled for peace and America went home to a new understanding of itself. Woodrow Wilson tried to make a lasting peace through the act of diplomacy. He failed miserably, however, as diplomats make terrible judges of history.

I should mention before I move on to the Great Depression that at about the time the war was winding down a furious flu epidemic swept the world and many millions died as a result of this disease. It was as if nature was showing mankind that no matter how evil he became he was still a pipsqueak when it came to true destructive power. To nature we owe a debt of gratitude for teaching us that few survive the onslaught of nature, war or no war. America and the world recovered from the flu and the war and all was restored for a decade or so as the world returned to the task of getting rich. One wonders why this generation was called upon to suffer so much, war, flu, depression, and then another war. Perhaps they were slow learners, or just plain unlucky.

The Great Depression

✦

(Or how not to get rich)

After the roaring twenties, a time of emotional indulgence after the depravations of war, America stood on the doorstep of lasting peace and prosperity. The last war had been fought, the economy was roaring, and prohibition was only a slight misstep on the path to chemical dependency. The trouble was, is, and always will be, that you can't finance the present out of the future for very long. Americans were making bank until the bank closed, the stock market crashed and the good times rolled on by. Margins and unwise loans had purchased false prosperity. Sooner, if not even sooner than that, the piper must be paid and those that have lived on the edge must fall off. America was living in the dreams of a tomorrow of good fortune. But oh what a nightmare the future turned out to be.

My family was caught in this hellish struggle of organized dust (man) running from real dust (Oklahoma). Nature had again turned its attention to this sorry generation and exacted a steep price. My family was poor before the depression; afterwards we were simply average. We slipped into the middle class as that class slipped down to join us. We had nothing all along and knew little else, but the middle class had known luxury and could not bear to live on so little as hope and prayers. But hope is a strange beast and finds a way to win in most situations. I give you the example of the great fraud exacted on the peoples of the dustbowl by unscrupulous Californians. Thousands of families left the dustbowl for the rich farmland of California and the promise of a new life and jobs. There were no jobs of course and the new life was little different than the old one, but odd as it may be, the hope of this band of foolish travelers did come true. In a far distant decade these wayward souls did find the Promised Land and so did their children, of which I am one. All this because most of them could not read, or at least could not read between the lines.

The great lesson of the depression was this. Your money is not really in a bank as many had supposed, it is out on loan, literally. Everyone can't take their money at the same time and so our great lesson was that to stabilize the country we must stabilize the flow of money, only you can't let the government do it alone or they will steal the public blind, and they will steal the public blind anyway, but it is far better that they aren't obvious about it. So we enacted legislation to protect our deposits and this has prevented the same stupidity from happening again. The depression was this country's second true example that democracy is not inevitably perfect, it only had the potential to be perfected. For American democracy is a subtle snake with two tongues, one for swallowing wealth and another for lying about it. The greater the lie the greater its chances for success in America. "Peace and prosperity in our time" was the motto. Death and war the result. Great depression? I ask. Lunatics running the Asylum, I respond. Feeding a lie causes a famine of the mind. The 1920's were all a great lie. Do not flatter history or those that made it in that hour, they were the fools of the century, next to the general public.

You may well be asking at this point how all this history belongs in a book about absurdity in our society. I will catch up to the present shortly, but we must all know whence we came from to have any idea how lost we are once we lose sight of where we are going. So, back to the depression. The depression was general madness on the grand scale, but poetry in the minor key of individual life. I read The Grapes of Wrath intensely, marking its similarity to my own family's history. I saw the faces of my own grandparents in the stories of the Joad family. We were the Joads, and so were millions of others. But my family moved on to Oregon and the green pastures of the Willamette Valley.

For this one act of courage I praise them, how would it have been if I'd grown up in California. I'd have never known the beauty of the rain and might even have a tan. And I'd be a Californian, not an American. I might even surf and play the mandolin, two of the noblest pursuits of the human species, next to living on a commune and eating off of food stamps.

My family made its way from the mid west to the far west via a truck that looked nearly identical to the one used in the movie "The Grapes of Wrath" only the Joads had a spare tire and a hood. My family quickly found that there were no jobs and kept right on going to Oregon, but not out of some incredible insight that their might be a better future there, but because my grandfather couldn't read and thought Oregon was a brand of gasoline. By the time his tank was finally full the family had crossed into the sweet soil of the Willamette. My family worked until they could purchase a farm of their own, and then worked themselves to death on it. The American dream is so beautiful. At any rate, that generation is gone now, having left a legacy of abuse, neglect, and alcoholism. Maybe God knew what he was doing with that bunch after all?

The Great Depression was a godsend for Americans. What better way to prepare for war than by practicing depravation? Unfortunately America went too far and elected Franklin Roosevelt president. He initiated almost all of the modern sins of poor government, including social security (nice idea but painfully flawed) and placing favorites on the Supreme Court, a decision that has paralyzed justice in this country. A man awarded a title on good graces soon loses his own goodness. And despite all of Roosevelt's efforts and infidelities the country only came out of the depression thanks to World War Two. If only we would have been patient this country could have been spared much misery. No government predicated on the principle that any citizen is entitled to anything long endures. We are entitled to our birthright, which is freedom of oppression from the government, and essentials such as food and clothes. Handouts beyond the essentials of life always squash the one beneath. The healthy are to heal the sick, not kill the disease.

I want to move on to World War Two, but a nagging sense that I've left out an important point is haunting me. Perhaps it will come to me as I stare out the window. Ah yes, here it is. The Depression is a lasting memory for those that lived through it, but we should always remember that it was caused primarily by greed. The Hawley-Smoot Act that plunged the nation into despair was aimed at preserving high profits for a privileged few (and Reed a Mormon no less, who supposedly had Divine inspiration in his decisions.) Apparently even God didn't see the stock market crash coming, what chance then had the sorry souls that lost their fortunes October of 1929. There will come again upon this land a second great depression, but it will be the forlorn Californians this time heading to Oklahoma in their BMW's and SUV's. Whining because they no longer can afford the price of a value meal. Brother can you spare a Perrier?

World War Two

✦

(Or the second war to end all wars)

Having left the Germans in poverty and humiliation after the war the nations of the world turned their collective heads toward Adolph Hitler and wondered how so crude and despicable a man could have possibly risen to power. Was this not the paperhanger of years past, they asked? Collectively Europe stood by and watched the Germans re-arm themselves though they were forbidden to do so. Then appeasement, a word that still bites into the flesh for the rawness of the cowardice it implies. All the while America played happily in its own backyard. The bully lived on someone else's corner. Chamberlain struggled to avert the war by giving the Germans whatever they wanted. But displaying weakness before a tyrant is the shortest road to slavery. And soon the world trembled at the mighty German war machine fueled not by diesel, but by the best scientists in the world.

America had no compunction to join in the fray that was rapidly turning bloodier than expected and the Germans had invented a new brand of warfare known as Blitzkrieg. We saw it more as a curiosity than a strategy, though we soon found out the terrible power of a Panzer division. We couldn't match the Panzers firepower until near the end of the war. Hitler idled his early war days by examining victory after victory. Then he made a terrible mistake, he decided to conquer Russia. Apparently Hitler was a terrible student of history because the one unalterable lesson from it is that Russia cannot be conquered, it can only be contained. It was for America a fortunate mistake for had he not made it an extra million Americans would have died fighting in the war. It is so much better, we believe, that that million were from a Slavic nation. Nonetheless, we entered the war because Hitler had a very stupid friend in Japan who believed he was as mighty as God. The Emperor believed he was descended from the gods, but more likely he was descended from the guards.

Pearl Harbor was the official beginning of the war for America. I've been to Pearl Harbor; it is a sad place. I mourned for the victims of the attack that was allowed to take place by a series of stupid acts followed by a few even more stupid tactics of the Japanese. Apparently, our own radar thought the planes were our own aircraft flying in that day from the mainland. The Japanese, after having sunk a few vessels, failed to attack the repair yard and the oil depot that supported them. Many people actually believe all those ships are still under the warm tropical water, only two remain, all the others were raised, repaired and put back into battle. The Japanese fell victim to one of the greatest logical errors of man, never wake a sleeping giant unless you blind him first. Pearl Harbor in the end was only a speck in our eye that was removed with blood. Once the giant awoke, the god trembled.

Of course we declared war on Germany at the same time we declared war on Japan. (Germany declared war on us first, but hadn't attacked.) Apparently, there is a law that states we must be at war with at least two countries at a time; otherwise I think this was shoddy reasoning and a great dupe upon the public. Roosevelt declared that December 7th, 1941 was a "day that shall live in infamy." It has, as a day we declared war on a country that hadn't attacked us, except our merchant fleet and they understood the risks. No one seemed at the time to question the reasoning. It was as if the Australian aborigines had attacked tourists with spears and our president declared, "I hereby declare war on Mars." Our preoccupation with the Germans caused the deaths of thousands of soldiers in the Pacific. A country should fight one war at a time or it risks two deaths.

The war dragged on and on and on, atrocities and death mounting by the hour. It is little comfort to note that we won the war realizing that we did little to stop it in the beginning. For all of our international clout we accomplished little more than verbal puffery, watching as England stood fast. England was Hitler's second big mistake. Never attack an enemy living on an island unless you possess the means to utterly destroy them. Where are they going to retreat to, think about it? England had no choice but to fight to the last man, and they nearly did. At the time of the cracking of the enigma code England was a few weeks from starvation. Hitler could never have sent a sufficient force across the channel to destroy a country so in love with their past. Brits would have died by the millions to preserve the cultural heritage they have lent to the world, mostly a small number of plays and poems. But especially good ones I assure you.

So Hitler, drunk on the murder and mayhem of his beloved Panzers, ultimately fell upon the sword of fate and attacked two undefeatable foes, the love of country and the insane love of country. Russia sacrificed untold thousands in the Battle of Stalingrad first and foremost because Stalin took it personally that his namesake had been attacked. He sacrificed row after row of foolish young men, who danced to their deaths either at the hands of the Germans or their own troops who shot them in retreat. This was insane, but those who shaped ultimate victory in Stalingrad were of course made heroes. As George Washington said, (and here I said he spoke so little) "You cannot defeat an idea with an army." Russia and England would never have been defeated at the same time. They cherished their country too much, and their lives too little. Notice the French lasted just a couple of days in the war, they weren't about to let their country be destroyed by mortar shells, they invited the Germans for supper and then waited for America and England to come and clean the dishes. The French were prudent; Paris is still beautiful in the spring, but what of Stalingrad?

But all good wars must draw to an end and the bedlam that had been spread across the face of Europe soon collapsed under the mass of too many fronts, too many enemies and too little time. The Americans and Russians raced to Berlin to capture the spoils of war, mostly German scientists required to produce nuclear weapons. Germany surrendered little by little as the Americans advanced from the west and Russia from the east. The German public was more inclined to surrender to the Americans given that the Americans weren't going to kill and torture them, but some of Germany fell into Russian hands nevertheless, leading to the Berlin Wall. The Berlin Wall was erected by East Germany to impede its inhabitants from walking over to the western sector fed by the Americans. Of course, the communists explained this by asserting they were just shooting the insane so they could be retuned for treatment. After all, who would want to escape from paradise, but the insane? It seems that there were scores of insane people in East Germany, and the guards were painfully poor shots as nearly all of the bullets aimed at inhibiting the crossings missed and killed the poor psychotics instead. Oh well, the cost of treatment was too high anyway.

Hitler had seen enough of the collapse of his vast empire and resolved to check out by putting a gun to his head and firing. Then he invited himself to a bar-b-que where he was the chief guest. Hitler recognized that the Russians would have tortured him and they undoubtedly would have. Though Hitler was perfectly prepared to toss a few Jews alive into a crematorium (yes, some were alive and kicking, not gassed first.) He himself opted for the posh position of dying beforehand. Fire then destroyed his remains, and the Third Reich, or "empire to last a thousand years" perished less than twenty years after seizing power. Perhaps the Third Reich's memory will indeed last a thousand years.

America then turned its total attention to the Pacific. Now if you recall what I said about islands you will be able to discern the difficulty in invading a country that would have defended itself to the last man. It would have cost America a million lives to invade Japan. Hence our humanitarian solution to the problem; vaporize hundreds of thousands of innocent people in order to save lives. Countries often speak in such double talk. Remember, the larger the lie and so forth. And in a case of "our German scientists are smarter than your German scientists" America dropped a bomb that obliterated certain unfortunates close to the center. Their remains are but shadows on the wall, and awfully tough to identify. So facing extinction at the hands of atomic energy the Japanese surrendered and Fascism died a quick death. Mussolini was also a part of the show, but he watched most of it from his dragged position to the rear of a horse, which was less than ideal.

America then took its place as the preeminent state on earth, but we paid a high price for waging war on Japan, they would one day charge us too much for their cars. This go round, however, we had learned our lesson and fixed the Japanese up properly with money and protection. Western Germany faired pretty well also. At last we had exposed the truth about victory, it is better shared among the vanquished than at their expense. We prospered after the war as much due to our wisdom in handling victory as in our skill in battle. But this was a long time past and America lost the sense of moral superiority it attained in the war. Our gallantry was forfeited in the jungles of Vietnam, the avenues of Kent State and the assassinations of the sixties. But temporarily, euphoria swelled across the land and Americans settled into a state of home and hearth and produced babies, lots of them. I was one of these post war tots. A generation doomed from the start by unreasonable expectations and the menace of nuclear holocaust. America became the vanguard of democracy and the cradle of family life. Only thing was, underneath the cradle flowed a current of despair two miles deep. America had won the war, but what was the prize?

VIETNAM

✦

(Or how not to run a world)

For a time in the early sixties it became crystal clear to a group of madmen, who worked at a secret castle called The Pentagon, that the world was being over run by communists. Now communists are the ogres that preach equal shares for all. This of course made them untenable in America, the land of the opportunity to grow up to be rich, so long as you are white. It seemed everywhere one turned a new country was adopting the creed of Marx and America resolved to take action, first in Korea and then in Vietnam. Now it occurred to no one that if democracy was indeed a superior system that by nature it would prevail in the long run, instead someone decided we needed to kill a hundred thousand schoolboys just to be sure we were right. And so we did. But somewhere in the insanity a few voices wailed that perhaps America the Great was mistaken. How could this be, we asked? Our judicious elders have said we must fight and so we did. Now we never actually won either war. Korea ended in a truce, similar to that word Armistice, so a line was drawn across the land and those that lived above it were made communists and those that lived below it were made democrats. The democrats had our total support. We had stopped the swelling of communism throughout the world. Or so we thought.

On the same side of the world another country became divided as to its future. Some folks fancying the opportunity to be rich like the Americans, though those numbers would be painfully few, and others wanting to divide what little they had among the people. Another war broke out. America sent advisors, then troops, in an effort to safeguard the world for democracy. The result virtually destroyed the country. You see, there is a grave difference between being asked to exchange blows to save your homeland, wives, mothers, sisters and children from a thundering horde and being asked to travel halfway around the world in an attempt to save a few people you never heard of from an ideology you have never read. This was especially hard to fathom for the nineteen-year-olds they asked to fight this war. They had no interest in Vietnam; few could spell it, fewer could place it on a map.

I remember those turbulent days clearly. The war protests on the campus of Oregon State University, the long hair, the rebellion, the draft dodging and freedom marching, but mostly I remember smoking pot, a lot of it. But the war dragged on despite our persistence and the youth of this country swam in a sea of doubt pertaining to the leadership of this country. Our leaders, we thought, were lying to us. Now our leaders had always lied to us, but it was different in the sixties because they allowed war correspondents to film and record the war and every night on the evening news the body count was displayed as families dined on TV dinners steaming in aluminum trays. The correspondents discovered the lies and sent word. Word got out and the country reeled. Eventually, the perpetrator of these horrific crimes was sent packing, albeit to a nice pension and a mansion on the seacoast of California. Richard Nixon was a liar who had the audacity to get caught. He wasn't good at it I suppose. Or as I might more readily believe, there were so many lies that not even the best liar on earth could cover them all up over a long enough period of time. Anyway, Richard fell and the country got up off its knees and battled back to prosperity and peace, which we then traded for cocaine, but that is another book.

I can sum up all that I know about Vietnam in one statement, if the middle class justly unites on any subject they are invincible. It was after the working stiffs joined the marches and protests that the war came to an end. America will never listen to its youth though its youth are often right, it will only listen to the man who signs the checks and that is Mr. and Mrs. Lunchbox. It is a shame that so many bright stars had to fall in Vietnam. I can scarcely stand to think of the memorial in Washington without the enormity of human folly and human waste washing over me. So many fine boys dead, fighting an enemy that ultimately committed suicide. Never fight for ideology, I say, only for preservation. In the end all ideas shall be replaced, even democracy. We are only the temporary custodians of a tiny light of hope. One day that light will blaze in full glory in a more enlightened age.

THE ASSASSINATIONS

◆

(Or how an idiot changed history)

In my youth there were actual leaders walking the land, men of passion, principle, valor, potent speech and a lust for the ladies. But hey, we all have our faults. I was and still am a big devotee of the Kennedy's and Martin Luther King. I grew up in an era when men spoke with such fervor it could thaw your heart. Nowadays most of the speeches involve a language I don't understand, doublespeak. It sounds similar to English but never betrays its country of origin. I believe, however, it came from an island nation called Coward. There isn't a single man in America with the courage to speak of his convictions. These men have all been killed politically by our penchant for unbearable scrutiny. The few whisper-white leaders that can withstand the onslaught of the press are only those holding no true convictions to be exposed. That way they can never be so wrong as to infuriate the public. Our price for letting the media gain so much power is a lack of true leadership in any endeavor other than business. We wanted freedom of speech and we got it. But no one seemed to understand that this meant that most speech would be inane. True leaders thrive only when they are not called to cower before every special interest group. However, we are not a nation united, but a conglomeration of groups that meet on the playing field of political battle once every four years to establish who has the most clout. I venture that any man that truly tried to change the world today would have to appear from prison. Who else has no reputation to lose?

I still remember the assassination of John Kennedy. I was seated in a second grade reading group when the principal blew in and relayed the President's passing to our teacher Mrs. Broccoli (yes she was named for a vegetable.) The horrific look on her face sent shivers down my spine. I didn't understand the true impact of President Kennedy's life until much later, but a dark wrenching in my gut led me to understand that my future was no longer quite as bright, or for that matter, the future of my generation.

It was after my last day in sixth grade that Robert Kennedy was assassinated. I loved the man. He ventured to my little town, Albany, only a week before his death. He left an impression on me that he could have changed the world. I believe it with all my heart. But our world was probably never meant to embrace the peace of simple human congregation. For as long as there are men that possess more than others there shall be strife, and death, and misery. And as long as there is one man that believes he is superior to his fellows there shall be greed and inequality. How truly rich we all could be, if only we chose to share. But it will never be so in a thousand years. We feel we must destroy the world in order to preserve our little advantages. One day we might all have nothing, because we wanted so badly to have more than another.

I often wonder what the world might be like today if these three men had lived. I can't say, not even God knows. But I can state that I might be different. I might never have lost my faith that I lived in a country that worshiped freedom, liberty and equality. I love America, don't get me wrong, but it's not the America I was assured so long ago. To those who have appeared in this world after the death of these men I say to you that once, for ever so flickering a moment, the world held out the hope of a better life. The idea was real, it was tangible. And when these souls departed this earth through the brutal hands of idiots, I lost my future and so did you. What those who did not live in the sixties have now in front of them is only a mere residue of what might have been. The rest has been plundered by fate.

THE COMPUTER AND THE
MODERN WORLD

✤

(Or how to break the world in two)

I t is an immense sadness to me that Bill Gates and I are exactly the same age, which means I had the same opportunity as he did to become the richest man on earth. I'd feel a lot better if he were older. But for everything given in this life something else must be taken, and I think that what was taken was Bill's soul. Thankfully, I still have mine. For no man on earth has had more power given to him to change the world and no man has ever done less to that end. All of his charity is but a drop in an endless sea, a toss of mortal bread to keep children from picking his wallet clean. Bill cares more about control than about the world, so he controls a part of the world, but not the part that matters. He doesn't control the thoughts of genius. As we look back upon past glorious states, such as Greece, we cannot name a single wealthy citizen unless we are told of his name by an author of the subject, but we can all name five philosophers, and perhaps a few mathematicians. What then of the wealthy? Well, I'm afraid their fame often terminates at death. Bill Gates will only be remembered as the head of a computer empire that didn't spot the sweeping change that toppled it.

However, I'm the first to admit the computer altered the world in a fundamental way. Before the computer (in those glorious days when counter help could count change) it seemed a great deal nobler to care about people. After the computer it seemed stupid to spend time stressing about people when there was so much space to explore in Cyberia, so much money to be made, so many games to be played. People could be created out of ones and zeros, no need to fuss over what will never change. But computers did change things. They changed them for the faster.

Our society today is a hodgepodge of the ultra fast and the too damn slow. We cringe if information takes longer than half a nanosecond to download. We rant and rave if someone isn't accessible by cell phone even if we call in the middle of the night. But for every person wired and tired there's another creature sitting contentedly in a rocking chair reading a first-rate book. America has become a land of the ultra new bounded by a cherishment of the very old. Even in the same house two mates aren't always in a matching electric bliss. One parks at the computer and analyses the stock market while the other stares at Jerry Springer and studies the lifestyle of a bizarre cult called "trailer trash."

I lie somewhere between these two worlds. I'm at this instant typing on a computer screen via a program by the identical company founded by the aforementioned Bill Gates. It rankles me that I've made him richer, but you know, I understand his programs and so do you, that is why he is so rich. I can't visualize myself typing on an old Corona and marking changes in ink above the tips of my words. So I'm excited by the electronic era so long as it permits me to be idle. Where I draw the line, and a lot of others do as well, is when the fascination is with the apparatus rather than with what it can do. My son is one such being; he lives to be in command of the machine, to program it, to maneuver an endless stream of ones and zeroes. I could care less. And this is our point of departure in the PC age. I still know how to add up change, he doesn't. I still read books, he never will. I can play actual games, such as basketball and softball, he plays video games. Now which generation is superior? Well, both are defective, but his world will be superior to mine, so long as war doesn't intercede. But I still remember the fascination of laboring over an equation with pencil and paper, of fondling paper money and chatting with smart clerks. I still remember the days of scribbling long hand and never-ending hours of penmanship and other pointless pursuits. When I think of it, my world sucked.

But where will all this data transmission take us as a nation? For all the computer's power, most of the world still uses Cyberia to download porn and e-mail endless chain letters to friends. The computer will only be a faster way of transmitting human stupidity if it doesn't transform people themselves. And has the computer transformed us? No, only the way we conduct our mindless pursuits. Much of the information on the Internet is available elsewhere, and usually in greater clarity, but I still use it, just not for learning. Oh, and lest I forget, the Internet is also used to disseminate misinformation, and downright lies. The Internet made the computer functional at last for the average person, but the only real change it has brought into our lives is the speed at which we may destroy our personal world. The computer is only an instrument by which we amplify our current desires. If that were the criteria by which we judge the computer's usefulness, then I say, toss the beige box in the trash and pick up a good book.

But despite my admonitions the computer is here to stay. I certainly have no desire to get rid of mine, except to update it of course, which must be done yearly, since new models are so much quicker at downloading information than last year's model. And besides, who would forward all those pointless chain letters. So I'll tap on, in hopes that the electric box will one day pull us from our sorry state into a nirvana of heavenly peace, but I think that is what I hoped for the television, and look where that has taken us. We as a people are easily bored. And evermore those wishing to prosper will find new ways to amuse us. It is my staunch hope that someday we will demand to be educated rather than informed by self-serving masters and demand of those appliances that are destined to govern our world that they make us more human after all. It is up to us to require the change. Las Vegas is richer than public television because we make it so. Bill Gates is richer yet because he foresaw the need for greater amusement and hungered to place a computer on every desk. Presumably, at least in public, his goal was to boost the productivity of the workplace. However, my wife just called from work, her boss is playing solitaire on his state of the art PC.

PAPER OR PLASTIC

❖

(Or could it be worse)

O f all the absurdities of modern life, little is more absurd than the ridiculous proposition offered at every purchase of "paper or plastic." Now what that statement is in fact saying is-by which method would you prefer to destroy the environment, cut down a tree or consume irreplaceable oil reserves. The odd thing is that we are given a choice, this is why. If the vendor truly had a passion as to saving the environment he would offer only the choice he thought best. What the vendor is saying by the offer is this-I'm too chicken shit to make a decision that might offend some of my customers and thereby lose them to my competition and subsequently lose my wife and kids to a superior earner, so I'll offer both and pretend I'm ethically anxious about the fate of planet earth. The truth is the vendor is only troubled about himself and his boat payment. I usually take plastic as my option of choice. I like the handles on the bags. I'd love to say it was due to my perpetual love of trees (and I do like trees) but in reality I make my decision based on far more mundane issues, such as how simple something might be to carry out to my car. Sometimes I take paper because the item is heavy and might tear through a plastic bag. I hope no one assumes because of this that I don't like trees. What I truly like is getting home, intact, all that I've bought with my hard earned money. So much for the environment.

I prefer to save the environment by not abusing the privileges of nature. I do not litter, I recycle, and I scowl at Californians who carelessly slump happy meal containers out their car windows. In short, I do practically nothing about the environment, but I feel good about myself for the effort I make. I do not donate money to any society purporting to save any of the endangered species in our world, nor do I sit in trees or lie down in front of log trucks, but I sometimes agree with those that do, unless of course it will cost me money due to their meddling. I care about the gas pump and the amount of fuel I burn unless I need to go someplace, then I care not at all. I care about the air I breath, unless the factory in town supports my business and allows people to buy my products. Do you see a quandary here? Everybody cares about the environment, in the abstract, but no one wants to be called upon to make the first official sacrifice for the cause. We all want our neighbor to go first, and then we will play along. Of course, nothing gets done, and little will ever get done until we have so abused our world that it seizes vengeance and kills us one by one. Of course if we're not the one we don't care. So polluters pollute until somebody prevents them, but no one will. It's not good for business.

Now back to plastic. Plastic was a brilliant idea at the time, but that was in an era when petroleum was both cheap and plentiful. No one refutes that plastic lasts a long time, that is the problem, it appears to last forever. It is a miracle that millions of year's worth of plant life first coalesces into the rich black tea that drives our world (no, oil is not the residue of dinosaurs) and then is burned or altered in an instant in our engines and refineries. We squander in mere moments what has taken millions of years to make. Does that seem wasteful to you? Of course not, gas is cheap. What is wasteful, we argue, is the heaping piles of plastic money we squander at Christmas, now that is a travesty.

I still hear the echoes of the check out clerk (once a high paid professional possessing great computational skills, but now a job that can be executed by anyone able to stand on two feet) hollering to his guest "paper or plastic." I assert to that fellow or lady, make a decision. Why is it always on my head as if I knew how best to spare the environment? And that is the whole of it; no one knows how to save the environment while pumping the economy at the same time. That is because you can't do both at the same time. I argue that the destiny of the world hinges on an impossible task, that of protecting the environment while keeping people fed and entertained. Impossible, I say. So the best course of action is to live free and die young. Those of us doomed to live into the next century will regret it, unless we are able to develop new technology that consumes less energy. And that suits me just fine so long as it is my neighbor bicycling in the rain while I straighten my tie in the mirror of my BMW.

AT THE MOVIES

✦

(Or I can't be king so I'll be famous)

F ew endeavors of American society have succeeded as well as our love affair with celluloid tape. We adore the movies, and what is even better; most of the world likes our movies too. A movie can double or triple its take on the world market. Then of course it's sold to cable, then to the video store and the tape buying public then to broadcast television, and I even left out pay-per view. With abundant options for making money it is a wonder that any movie ever loses any, yet they frequently do. Sometimes movies are brilliant, sometimes they are horrible, but often they are a little of both. I too, like the vast majority of my cohorts, love the movies. I like to rent them for home or go to the theatre in the afternoon and watch the latest films in private. But I even find solace in bad movies. I love the places the movies take me since I'm too poor to travel. Occasionally the setting is as important as the star, but what is always true is that the story is only of minor importance (you tell me American Graffiti had a storyline?) In fact the screenwriter gets about the same credit for the success of a movie as does the set caterer. Several screenwriters are highly paid, but that is an accident, the majority of screenplays are drivel, turned into genius at times by the skill of the director. I offer one exception "Chinatown", which was a brilliant screenplay, turned into a bloody bore of a movie by a boob of a director.

What I love the most about the movies are of course the actresses (actors are tolerated if they are playing a good role in a movie with lots of actresses). I believe the most gorgeous women in the world work out of Hollywood. I live in a fair sized town, but I seldom see such woman walking my streets as those that stalk the silver shadows of the movie theatre. If Nicole Kidman lived next door I'd spend all day outside eager to see her, or if Alicia Silverstone worked in the cubicle next to mine, I might never work, but alas they are fictions as much as the characters they play. In real life these lovely ladies are as mundane as any women I've known in my time. Everyone is lovely, made up and in good light. Even Halle Berry needs a little help, but very, very little.

The standard plot of all movies is basically this-a character who is rough on the exterior but possesses a heart of gold, gets himself into a good deal of mischief and spends approximately two hours getting out of it, oh, and along the way he or she gets laid. This formula has survived the comings and goings of multiple generations and shows no sign of changing. The beauty of this plotline is that it plays well all over the world. The Academy Awards show attracts nearly a billion pairs of eyes each year; more people than worship the Pope as the Vicar of Christ. But the movies had a better year. The majority of the top grossing movies are action pictures requiring millions of dollars to make and millions of dollars to promote. These movies usually necessitate the employment of one or two "bankable" stars to attract a sizeable opening weekend audience. There are exceptions to action pictures, but precious few. "Forrest Gump" is an exception, but lets not forget it employed Tom Hanks, our countries finest dramatic actor (thankfully, he tossed his early penchant for comedy) so it had a chance to be good by that fact alone. It made hundreds of millions of dollars and contained, I believe, only one violent action scene, the slaughter of thousands of innocent shrimp.

About once a year a movie comes to the screen that is beautifully crafted, well-acted, well directed, and has an utterly incomprehensible storyline. This movie is usually rewarded with an Academy Award nomination or even several actual awards. "The English Patient" is a perfect example (if you can explain this movie to me you're smarter than Einstein.) Hollywood appears to adore the serious film even if it makes no sense. Each year, come awards time, we are presented with at least one movie we never heard of, and which lasted less than a week at the theatres, that is now being proclaimed as a labor of genius. This baffles us outsiders because we are simply unaware and are caught off guard. After the ceremony we are presented a second chance to view the film, thanks to its Oscar publicity, and we flock to the theatre in hopes of discovering a hidden treasure. Of course, we are bored to tears, but now the movie has the Academy's stamp of approval so we concoct nice things to say and dream up clever witticisms about our profound understanding and appreciation of the movie's "craft," which is all bullshit. Then we return to the action pictures we love and watch an assortment of items get blown to bits and feel soothed somehow by this.

However, the most fascinating facet of the movies is not the movies themselves but the power movies have to create some of the most famous human beings on earth, next to television stars. More people can name the star of "Terminator" than can name the President of the United States, but again, Arnold had a better year. In our country of equals and lack of royalty Hollywood has worked as an ample substitute for our hunger to worship something greater than ourselves, though that something is a part of us. You see, actors and actresses are no different than you and me; in fact a lot of them have served our morning coffee or dished up our well-done steaks as we dined unawares. Most actors and actresses are also waiters and waitresses because, as you might imagine, there is an extended waiting list of people coveting a piece of the royal lineage.

A famous actor or actress is more famous than the royalty of Europe or the heads of state since the movies have this hypnotic influence over our common sense. These people also are filthy rich and live lives we commoners can only imagine. So there are many more applicants for the job of fame than there are seats at the royal table. Every so often a phenomenon comes along and knocks a veteran out of his preferred seat, usually by selling a great deal of movie tickets, but by and large each generation produces twenty to twenty five gifted actors and actresses who then dominate the landscape for a decade or so until they too are felled by the fickle ax of fame and are relegated to portraying mothers and fathers of the newly famous, or crotchety old folks in general.

And why you ask are we so in love with the stars of the movies? I believe it is due to the fact that we feel actors are our friends, neighbors, family, and loved ones all wrapped into one gorgeous package and laid before our eyes in wide screen splendor. We know these people on an intimate basis. Their nose hairs are a foot long on the screen, we know their intimate parts and touch the inner workings of their hearts and minds due to their skill in conveying emotion, in short, they are everything the majority of the people we know are not. So we fall in love at the movies and want a piece of the star for ourselves. We make them more famous than they should be and hope to meet them one day, though most of them would rather not meet us. I've only seen, in person, two or three famous people. They had to be pointed out to me, but I thought they would glow in the dark or something to that effect.

EDUCATION

✦

(Or how to get ahead while going deep in debt)

The state of education in this society is at a crossroads. College is too expensive as the need for a college degree is at a premium in our ever more technological country. So now, in our present, enlightened age, each and every student (except the offspring of the rich, and do they really need college or just an inheritance) must go deep into debt to afford the wonders that a piece of sheepskin can supply. It is not uncommon for a professional graduate to go into the job market a hundred thousand dollars in debt, or more. That should mortify us, but it doesn't because many of these debt-ridden souls will soon be out earning us and living in superior houses, all the while driving BMW's as we struggle to keep up the payments on our Hyundai. So into debt they go, most never to return.

I myself went deep into debt to finance a degree in despair from a public university. I'm afraid I didn't grasp the difference in perception in a degree from Harvard and a degree from a facility with the name "state" attached at the end. Oh well, I never really liked the rich anyway. My tiny piece of diploma with the words Bachelor of Political Science across it has provided me with a modest income and an even more modest net worth. But I take great pride in the fact that I "went to college." So did Bill Gates, however he left to become a billionaire. (I wonder if being a quarter million dollar in debt qualifies for some special name)? In short, my diploma is still in a box in my garage where it is now doing about all the good that it has ever done.

But there is a true dilemma brewing in the back streets of America. What of those that sink into the abyss of debt then go on to teaching or other penniless pursuits? How will we get people in the future to go fifty thousand in debt in order to accept a teaching post that pays twenty nine thousand to start? It will get harder, if not impossible, to train the next generation. Not that they are very well trained now, but they do get diplomas. Do we really need college educated store clerks or box boys? What we need are highly trained professionals, but there are only so many positions to fill and so many colleges to fill them. But as the price increases, along with the wages of those who finish school, the desire for the diploma increases to the point practically everyone is willing to sink into debt to finance their future. Shouldn't the government help? They do, but not nearly enough.

In my lonesome, heartbreaking four years at a public facility I paid in the neighborhood of three thousand dollars in tuition and perhaps another thousand in books and fees. But I came out of the experience twenty two thousand in debt. Now you may be asking-what the hell did he spent the rest of it on? And the answer is of course, playing poker and losing. (Okay, only some of it.) But I had a family to support, a house payment and two cars. I borrowed to pay bills while I treaded water at school. This because of some poor advice I once gave myself that I didn't need to go to college straight out of high school. I told myself to wait until I was ready. Well, I became ready at the ripe age of twenty-five. Never take advice from yourself when you are dead wrong, this is what I learned in school. But today a student of even modest pursuits such as a Bachelors Degree in English is eager, ready and able to accumulate thirty or forty thousand in debt. Now I could tell them that if they took that money and invested it in stocks they would be richer in thirty years than if they went to school, but the young never listen, do they?

I propose the modest suggestion that we stop funding college and set up all of our young people as carney's until they possess enough sense to appreciate the hard-earned money we squander on them. Perhaps we can petition Congress? However, the harsh truth is they will never appreciate the hard-earned money we spend on them until they are older and it is their hard-earned money being spent on their kids. But I do think the carney idea is an excellent one. I just called my twenty-year-old son and informed him the circus is still in town. Alas, you have grander delusions that your child will go off to college, earn a degree, cure cancer and make you painfully proud in the process. Of course, he or she goes off to school, gets into financial trouble, drinks too much, gets pregnant, runs off to Africa or any of a multitude of other diversions. And these are the good kids. Wouldn't it be wiser just to send them off for a few years until they grow some concern for their future? I hear a ship sailing for the Gold Coast even as I write.

Seriously (if indeed I can be serious) we as a country need to reevaluate the educational process we squash our children into. I believe that we should stop taking summers off, graduate kids at sixteen, then send those that wish off to two years of vocational training, and those that have the desire and potential off to four years of legal suffering at a university. This would produce more working years in which to pay off the debts so accumulated and take aimless teenagers and place them in a goal oriented world, which would allow them a meaningful future. For the rest of the kids (those that hate school) my rich, educated children will always need a place to knock over milk bottles in a vain attempt to win a cupie doll for a girlfriend or boyfriend that doesn't love them.

SPORTS

✦

(Or how I made millions though I can't
read or write)

Nothing can, or has, captured the imagination of our society like sports. We love all sports from football to Battle Bots. It doesn't even have to be a game that makes sense, such as cricket. If it appears on television we watch, if it comes to town we buy a ticket. Now our insatiable appetite has created some great absurdities. While a school teacher with a masters degree earns 40,000 a year, Alex Rodriguez makes that sum per swing of his bat even though seven out of ten times he makes an out, not bad work if you can get it. And why do we pay star athletes a king's ransom? Because they help us to win, which in the end accomplishes nothing for society, but does help us pass time on weekends. An owner may spend countless millions on payroll to get a winning team, but sometimes that strategy backfires and what he gets is a gang of egotistical whiners. But every so often a bona fide winner emerges, and for this winner the owner is prepared to sacrifice almost anything, even most of the profits, in order to make him appear a winner in our society. After all, he succeeded in business why not in sports, though the two are as opposite as opera and rock.

I follow sports as closely as anybody, particularly college football, which I proclaim as the greatest of all sports, but I know when to draw the line on stupidity. I don't fritter away six or seven hours a day watching sports or donate a half million dollars to my favorite university's team (as if I had the choice) but I do purchase season tickets to my alma mater's games and watch the replays of every fall weekend's events. In the winter I take a break and only follow college basketball (with football, I've been known to watch a junior high game or two, I love the game, period). In the summer I limit myself to following just one local baseball team, although by local I'm afraid I mean two hundred miles away. I live in Oregon and professional sports is limited to one local basketball team that fits into the category of whiners rather than winners, though they are owned by one of the richest men in the world who happens to be a buddy of THE richest man in the world. So I wander in and out of the sports landscape like a bobcat on patrol. I seldom listen to sports talk or to shows about sports, this seems absurd to me, but to each their own.

What shocks me most about the sports scene in America is that no one seems to mind that the millions of dollars these gentlemen and ladies earn comes out of our pockets in the form of exorbitant ticket prices. The ticket buying public pays these outrageous salaries; the owners simply sign the checks. And why don't we mind that some athletes earn more in a day than we do all year. Is it because we love to win, because we have won so little in our personal lives? It is glorious to support a winning team even if our loyalties are as fickle as a September breeze. I know men that root for a different team every year and even one or two men that will jump ship halfway through the season. They want to win, end of story.

I, however, prefer the loyalty of the college game. I went to a public university that fields a team in one of the top conferences in the nation. It was a tremendous thrill as a boy to watch such luminaries as O.J. Simpson (pre White Bronco days), Pete Maravich (before his heart attack), Lew Alcindor (before he became a Muslim with an unspellable name), and John Elway (before his knees made him slower than me) all arrive into our little valley, our village of 50,000, and play a game or two. We even won on occasion; in fact the only college football game that O.J. did not score a touchdown in was a game played in Corvallis, Oregon in November of 1967. Unfortunately, it was our last victory over that team until the fall of 2001.

I had the grave misfortune as a boy to watch the successful Oregon State teams of the late 1960's. I became hooked for life. Little did I know I'd be called upon to endure twenty-eight consecutive losing seasons including one season where we won no games at all. Talk about loyalty. I paid for tickets year after year. I attended, sweated, fumed and occasionally screamed for joy with my team that I loved though they made the game as futile as a Mandela building session at a Buddhist temple. To love the Beavers was a Zen-like experience of learning to find joy amid suffering. I endured myriads of games with scores like 60 to 0, 52 to 14, and so on and on and on. We couldn't compete, but it didn't matter as far as my loyalty was concerned. I stayed strong, resolute like a flock of nuns at an army outpost. I loved my team, hell or high water, and low and behold as I passed through the various stages of life I came to middle age to find that my team at last had found a way to win. Words cannot describe the joy of our first winning season. It was a heaven only a chosen few were invited to attend. I'd endured the suffering, the humiliation, the discouragement and had been rewarded with a dream season that defied all description. Name me a professional team that has ever inspired so much loyalty as your own alma mater. Go Beavs!

However, no discussion of sports in America would be complete without mentioning the rise of women's sports. Now why do women want to play sports, because they want to get rich like the men? Maybe one or two actually like to play for fun, but I don't know these two individuals personally. And don't get me wrong, there is nothing wrong with trying to get a piece of the pie, especially when the pie is utterly gigantic and covered in greenbacks. I applaud women for standing up for their rights and demanding equal funding. Countless thousands of women have gone to college on scholarship and even a few onto professional sports, although these teams are still few and far between. Women still make a lot of money in golf and tennis, though they have always been allowed to participate in both sports. It was only when women wanted to play basketball, softball, volleyball, soccer and

other ostensibly manly sports that society got into a hullabaloo. However, women did things the American way and sued the NCAA for
their rights, and they won. But how absurd it is that a people, particularly a majority people as women are in this land, have to sue their own
government to get rights that should have been theirs all along.

I remember the battles over Title Nine and even the struggle to get
high school sports added for girls, it was argued that women couldn't
play the game well enough (well, how do you get good when you never
play?) and that it would lead to a unisex society (and what is so bad
about that?) In the end all these arguments proved futile and America
entered a new world where girls could get their dads to scream just as
loud at their games as when their sons played. There are now even
some sports where women outdraw men such as gymnastics. It can
only be argued that if sports are good for men and society then they are
equally good for females. Although now the females must come to
terms with such societal expectations as winning at all costs, coaches
who cheat to win and universities that care little for them once their
eligibility expires. Ah, but what a glorious new age. So when will
women's professional football be coming to town? And I understand
Ali is boxing at the Rose Garden on Saturday, his daughter that is.

THE POOR

✦

(Or how to get by with nothing, or even less)

I think Jesus said it best when he said, "the poor you will always have." That is a safe bet, for as long as there are unscrupulous people, liars, cheats and cons there will be the poor. And it is as sure as the sunrise that we will always have those kinds of people. It is worked into our psyche that the poor are to blame for their own woes. This is about as true as the myth of the Leprechauns. The poor are basically those people whose talents and skills are diminished by a population of baboons who believe that their ability to speak or compute or operate otherwise expensive equipment is valued far more on the open market than the modest skills of being kind, or neighborly. I've met the poor, the actual poor who live in the sleaziest area of Portland Oregon. I've been inside many of their homes to sell various products. I've seen how they live, how they think, how they judge, how they love. If you think you are somehow superior to these folks because you work at Intel or Tektronix you are a depressing human being. I've seen more of simple human decency in these homes than in all of the suburbs combined.

I've seen poverty's face. Trust me, it is demoralizing and debasing to those who must suffer its wrath. Families are broken, homes are broken down, lives shattered, self esteem abused and pain and misery abound in the kingdom of the poor. Yet we ignore them because they do not speak at us with the same volume that we speak to them. If they did we would listen. Because they are quiet we assume they are well. But believe it or not (and most of you don't) almost ninety per cent of the American population is ninety days from poverty should a paycheck cease to be forthcoming. Ninety days isn't a great deal of division between the suburbs and the wrong side of town. And there are those that sometimes venture back and forth between these two worlds as their means grow and diminish. I live in the suburbs now, but I did live two weeks in my car. (Okay, my wife threw me out and took my money). I crawled out of my hole because someone let me out. I'm white, educated, possess morals and values, communicate effectively and otherwise possess what society says it takes to earn a decent living, but I've been inside homes where the breadwinner has never earned more than half my current salary though he is equally adept at living a good life. The answer to poverty is simple, let the people out.

Do not involve yourself in programs and endless entitlements, do not immerse yourself in community actions or in literacy campaigns, do not strive to end injustice and income inequality unless you are first willing to let the people out. Open the cages of the poor and let them run in the street, let the sick be healed, let the lame walk, let the opportunity be sent, let the invitation to wholeness be given, to all men, now and forever, to do less than this robs all men of their own freedom. Have you never learned this? Has no one ever stood up in front of your face and laid bare the obvious truth. For every man that bolts the door closed to the poor creates another type of poverty, the poverty of the soul. America is the poorest nation I know. Yet others say we are rich. I don't feel rich, I feel comfortable, and there is a huge disparity between the two. I've opened the gates to the poorhouse and let the demons of hell loose upon the world. I will not be poor anymore and I will not make another man poor anymore. Everyone must be given the keys of the kingdom or else the earth will drown in its own filth. I've cleaned my house, now clean yours.

Okay, that was my feeble stab at being serious, and I succeeded I think. Poverty is one subject I just can't stomach. There are only poor because there are people in the world willing to enslave others. No man is free until all are free. Money is only a tool, it can be used to pry open the human heart or to seal it shut forever. Choose your weapon in the war against poverty. I've chosen the pen, for though it may not be mightier than the sword it is a potent deterrent to tyranny. Tyrants love poverty, almost as much as unlimited power. "The poor you will always have" the carpenter said. Yes, and greed and covetousness too. For where there is one the other sins will follow.

BLACKS AND WHITES

✦

(Or how I learned to love grits)

I was born into a town of almost pure white blood. We had one black family that moved into town when I was in junior high school. I'd never seen a black person up close before, only at a distance while driving through the streets of north Portland. My first taste of integration came on the football field. This black youth, whose name I cease to remember, walked onto the field, though the season was almost in full swing, and was straight away made starting halfback. I found this peculiar, he hadn't asked to be a halfback or any kind of back, but he was black, so my coaches assumed he could run. But there were one or two slight problems. First, he could sprint all right, at a snail's pace. Second, he couldn't keep from fumbling the football when hit hard. Yet in spite of these obvious shortcomings it took two or three games before he got benched. So my first experience with the black community was one of optimism. All my coaches had hoped this kid could run and thus turn our school into the winner it had forever strived to be. But alas, all hope was dashed in a few open field tackles that stripped us of our chance at victory.

The sad fact was this-the poor kid was ever after just a black kid in an all white school. He didn't fit. I don't consciously remember anybody making overt racial slurs or in any manner openly taunting him, but he wasn't special so he was ignored. His family moved away about six months later and they never came back. Over time a few new black families moved into town, perhaps lured by the high tech industries of our bordering university town, but this happened long after I'd moved to the big city of Portland and learned of a new world I'd only read about in books. I had to approach face to face a colony of people whose lives diverged from my own on roads I'd never fathomed to exist. I had to meet the black community on their own turf and survive, much as they must survive in my world, though they are seldom invited into it.

I'd been taught soundly and possessed at my first encounter with black society a mind primed and pumped to dispel all the myths that had been beaten into my head by a society shackled in racism. I believed that all men were free at heart and there was little difference between black and white save the pigmentation in their skin cells. So it was that after employment by a large pest control company I was sent straight from the backwater of Albany (white bread) Oregon into the heart of darkness (literally.) I knocked on a ramshackle door and could never have been prepared for what lay beyond. A young black man, late twenties, answered the door dressed in pajamas sporting four huge holes in the bottoms and a pair of slippers with long black toes peeking out the ends. He squinted at the vivacity of the sun though it was straight up noon on a summer day. If I'd been told I was standing in the middle of Mississippi I would have believed it. He beckoned me into the house and the smell of crusty carpet and antique linoleum all but made me vomit.

In the living room, filled with three overstuffed sofas with little stuffing, I found eight young black men sleeping on sofas although, I repeat, it was straight up noon. Two or three of them twisted and moaned as I spewed words out of my mouth with great ferocity eager to alleviate the tension in my body. The young man who had answered the door nodded his head as he escorted me to the kitchen, which reeked of rancid grease and week old supper. He showed me an ancient stove pinned against a decaying wall. He motioned for me to inspect behind the black body of the stove so I positioned myself to his left and clicked on my high-beamed flashlight. A thousand cockroaches (no I didn't actually count them) scurried in a struggle of life and death back into a crack in the wall. I turned green at the gills and said something stupid like "geez." He recanted the whole history of the cockroach problem from the day his family had first moved in twenty years prior. He had just inherited the house from his mother who had just died and he desired to eliminate the cockroach problem once and for all, though I told him he would have to burn the place to actually accomplish this. He seemed unperturbed by the six hundred-dollar price tag and promptly signed the papers for the treatment.

I strolled back across the strewn bodies, some of which had moved, alleviating my fear that some of these folks might be dead. My host slipped into a sleeping bag near the front door and asked if I might close the door behind me on the way out. I smiled, pleased about my first sale in Portland, and slipped out the front door with nary a glance. My first experience in the black world was over, but what, I thought, had I just experienced? I'd entered an island of humanity that hadn't dispelled the myths of my youth, but had reinforced them. Had I been wrong? I drove back to the office uncertain if I had the fortitude to continue. I wanted the suburbs again.

I drove back to the office, shaken, and thought to tell my boss I couldn't hack north Portland. I'd experienced the awful truth about poverty and all the stereotypes of black culture were true. I felt ashamed. I'd held to the unconditional belief that I was above racism, yet I'd judged an entire culture based on one experience. I believe that is the reason for racism's existence. Too many people in our society judge other cultures based on limited and distorted information. One visit into north Portland and I'd seen the horrible truth. Black people, especially men, were lazy. They were unconcerned for their health and welfare, they lived in squalor and young black men had no ambition and slept until noon. I went home that night and longed to never leave the suburbs again. Nevertheless, I was destined to pay plenty of visits to north Portland over the next year and discovered a few new things about human beings, some of which happened to be black.

Like all brainless people I'd jumped to a few conclusions. First conclusion, that the experience of my first visit was characteristic of all encounters. I thought it was typical for black people to sleep until noon. But from that first visit I never saw anybody still in the rack after noon, at least no black people. Over time the truth was revealed in an odd, diabolical way. One day I was called to a different house around the corner from the ramshackle house and the lady just happened to know the young man who owned it. It turned out all the young men living there worked a graveyard shift at a warehouse and were living in the house out of the generosity of the owner. His sole desire was to help other young men save money to buy homes, get married and raise families. I hadn't met a slovenly black man on my first visit I'd met a true hero. I believe Men are the most foolish the moment they pronounce themselves most wise. We are all so ignorant of the left hand of society that we are often made the folly of history, in due course and after many tears at our hands.

SMOKING OR NON

❖

(Or how to die trying)

There are not just the divisions of race in our society, but also the divisions of the do's and don'ts. Sometimes the do's are on the side of right and sometimes the don'ts are the most politically correct, such as those who don't have unprotected sex. The do's are usually right when right involves an action, the don'ts when it involves slovenly behavior. But no one act so polarizes the do's and don'ts so much as smoking. I'm so used to hearing smoking or non in a restaurant I simply nod when the correct word is spoken and the hostess more often than not reads my head tilt perfectly. She can tell the difference even without a burning butt in my mouth. Smokers are now in the minority, thanks to the American Cancer Society and the truth, which is that smoking kills most everyone including those unlucky enough to live with a smoker. Second hand smoke is a relatively new term that has fed the fire of division more than any one subject. For who should die at the hands of a smoker, except the smokers themselves? But others die in droves and that is unjust, even most smokers agree with this statement.

I smoked my first cigarette at the age of fourteen. I had no natural addiction to nicotine so it was not to inhale the deadly poison that I first lit up. In fact I'd done it for the same reason that everyone lights up, because movie stars looked cool doing it. My friends thought that I might look cool doing it as well. And I actually thought at the time that I did look cool. But I coughed at first, cool came later. Cool is an acquired state and no man who imitates another is in fact cool, cool is a byproduct of originality. But sometimes the true soul has a few destructive tendencies and doesn't live long. Cool at times is a death wish manifested in some less obvious way, such as driving at ninety miles an hour and taking a car head on. Nonetheless, cool is brief, even if the true soul lives on. Cool leaves us when our desire to live exceeds our desire to die. So I lit my first butt in hopes of being cool. I was prepared to pay any price, and some folks I know have already laid down their lives in the quest for cool. But cool leaves us, in life or in death. So why not live, why is living not the coolest thing?

I started by smoking a popular brand known as "Marlboro." It was advertised as the preference of rugged cowboys and gunslingers. Only I wasn't told that many years earlier it had been a woman's cigarette and the only thing that had changed was the advertising. But I was fourteen and easily duped. We are much too sophisticated today to fall for such palpable ploys, (strong enough for a man, yet made for a woman.) I smoked Marlboro's for four years before motivation prompted me to quit and then I promptly gained twenty-five pounds, which is why many souls don't quit even though they would have to weigh four hundred pounds to equal the health desolation of smoking. Better to look thin in the coffin, they think. All smokers should be forced to watch a person die from emphysema. The person reposes in a deathbed and hacks up bits and pieces of their lungs while writhing in agony from the pain that is so immense not even morphine can deaden it. Now talk about cool.

When I first started smoking I paid twenty-five cents for a pack out of a vending machine, machines that could plainly be found anyplace including fast food restaurants and small grocery stores. The point of vending machines was of course to sell the product to kids who couldn't legally buy cigarettes at the store, where cigarettes could be bought for less than two dollars a carton. One and all turned their heads at minors buying cigarettes, it was seen as harmless or just as a bad habit. Now it is a lot harder for minors to buy smokes, they have to ask their parents to get them. But the hardest part is coming up with the ransom money to buy them. A pack of cigarettes can cost up to four dollars a pack. Now it has always seemed absurd to me to plant a burning stick in your mouth and then to breath the excrement into otherwise pink lung tissue, but it is extraordinarily absurd to buy a product for an outrageous amount of money that ultimately kills you without remorse and to think all the while you look cool doing it. What you are is on a collision course with death. How cool are corpses?

However, second hand smoke is the true absurdity in the smoking world. When I was younger it was unheard of to ask a smoker to smoke outside. It would have been an outrage. How dare you, I can still hear the smokers howling. But times change and science marches on. Now it is well known that just standing in the vicinity of a smoker causes a person to suffer debilitating effects. Some, or perhaps most, have died from this unwitting falsehood carried to us by the tobacco companies that are among the best liars to have ever lived (they could even teach presidents a new wrinkle or two.) Smoke in any form is unhealthy; it seems incredible to me that I even need to write this. It is like saying hydrochloric acid isn't healthy to drink. Smokers have now been relegated to the alleys, the street corners, the decks and the porches of America. The majority has spoken and pronounced that tobacco is a crime of sorts, a crime of stupidity, but should we be punished for stupidity, I ask? Yes, why else. How bizarre that our own bad habits can kill others though they don't partake in our actions. This is an oddity of life, yet painfully poetic in its injustice.

Today we have certain states, such as California, that have banned all smoking in public places. Others have banned smoking only in public facilities, but restaurants and bars may adopt their own individual policies. Smokers howl discrimination, and they are right. We have doggedly striven in this country to segregate the undesirables. But smoking is an option and not a burden of birth and since non-smokers are the majority, the majority rules, and breathes, with its fiery will. I picture the day when smoking will be practiced with the same regularity as bloodletting is today. It will be viewed as crass and vulgar, which

it is. And no one will be predisposed to pay the thorny taxes on cigarettes. I need a pack of smokes, I hear a future man saying, can you
cover change for a hundred? Why indeed, a future grocer states, here's
your fourteen cents. I'm glad I quit, but I still draw in wisps of smoke
as I stand in the streets downtown and mull over the long pull of a
Marlboro. Then I count my change and grasp that I've saved almost
twenty thousand dollars by quitting and feel much better.

PRISONS

✦

(Or how to bend invisible bars)

We as a society erect a great many prisons to house the unfortunates that happen to get pinched during the commission of a crime or who are later convicted beyond a reasonable doubt in a court of law. But are all prisoners convicted under the same tenants of law or are some handed a heavier sentence due to the prejudices of the jury? And are some convicted even though innocent by a prosecutor hell bent on convicting somebody, anybody, of the crime. The answer is yes. Justice in our country is a slippery concept. We preach justice for all, but what we truly mean is justice for all persons we like, the rest can rot in hell. Today prisons are increasingly high tech, involving less and less human contact to dispense food, medicine and recreation. It seems the greatest absurdity to me to place a young man in a situation where he is destined to fail. Whatever happened to the penitence part of penitentiary?

We have adopted a tough on crime policy of late. Build more prisons, make more laws that can be broken, incarcerate prisoners for longer terms and execute those that kill. I concur with some of this. Capital crimes require great punishment because what has been taken cannot be replaced; a lost life is just that-lost. But what of individuals whose crimes are against property, should they be dumped in the garbage heap of humanity and written off as doomed to failure? Of course not! We seem as a society to begrudge the prisoner even the simplest of vital tools to cope with the outside world. We consign the prisoner to a cell with a master thief and then tell him, six or seven years later, to go out and learn a trade. Well the only trade he has learned in prison is to steal, and he has learned his lessons well. It is the fact that this person was denied fundamental needs in his personal life that he took to crime in the first place, whether that be love or material goods, or parents, so we place him in prison and then deny him even what little he has been begrudged in his life. Afterward we toss him on the street and say, good luck. Ridiculous.

I read in the papers almost daily of a prisoner in a far off state released after twenty years in prison for a crime he didn't commit. Thanks to the availability of DNA testing we now are more assured of a person's guilt than in the past. But doesn't it frighten you that so many juries have convicted in error. The time for juries to decide cases has past and it is now time for cases to be decided by a panel of three judges who hear the case on its merits then permit the accused an appeal. The concept of "a jury of your peers" had its place, but now there is no such thing in all the world. Anyone with a little sense avoids jury duty however it is possible to do so. So what we are left with are those lacking the sense to be removed from the task. This is a jury of your peers? Not at all. Juries can cave in to the temptation to trust the unbelievable as they enter the courtroom with a catalog of prejudices and precepts without veracity. Why do you think lawyers spend so much time on jury selection?

We'll refuse a young man a few thousand dollars to pursue an education or to get schooling in a field of interest, but have no compunction whatever spending a hundred thousand dollars housing him in a prison that assures the death of his future. His prison record hangs around his neck like an albatross. There is no paying of one's debt to society unless that debt is also forgotten. Criminal records have their place, especially due to the fact so many prisoners repeat their offences, but is that due to a lack of contrition or to a lack of attention by society? I say spend our money saving the young rather than destroying them. The annual budget of the Oregon State Penitentiary would pay for room and board and tuition for every prisoner at a private college.

Lets send them all there and see what happens, only lets do it before they commit the crimes that rob them of their life.

I lived in Crescent City, California at the time of the opening of Pelican Bay State Prison. It is a technological marvel, allowing for the barest of contact between prisoner and guard. It was designed to house the worst of the worst, the true incorrigibles. Its rigid steel and concrete exterior creates a sharp contrast to the splendid redwoods that surround it. At the time assorted states and local principalities sent emissaries to the prison to study its secrets; to learn how to control prison populations that were growing ever more violent. Everyone in the country was striving to be the toughest; no one was striving to be the most humane. We often forget in this country that the punishment for the crime is the actual incarceration. We are under no right to debase the prisoner any further than that.

Now it is hard to possess sympathy for a man who has brutally raped a twelve-year-old girl and scarred her for life. I have no sympathy whatever for those actions. We read of these acts and believe no punishment harsh enough to compensate for the loss. But what we fail to realize is that there was a day before that act occurred and it was in that day society failed. We must reach the young before they commit the crimes; afterwards there is no course but retribution. And don't think for a minute that our soaring prison population isn't due to past racism. We will always pay a price for keeping a man in the gutter even if that price is just in gazing at the gutter as we drive past. When we as a society impoverish a segment of that society it will cost us more in the end than if we simply allowed them the equality they deserve. How much better would our country be if we didn't send such a high percentage of black men to jail? Wouldn't their families be better off, especially their children, if dad were simply granted a decent opportunity to earn a living?

It is in our collective wisdom that we feel justified in sending violent criminals to prison, but these acts say as much about ourselves as they do about the prisoner. We will stand by and watch a young man or woman enter a life of drugs and poverty and say nothing. But the day that child acts on the hatred and neglect he feels we pounce on his head with the full wrath of indignity. Where is the prison wherein we punish ourselves for our societal misdeeds? It is in the graveyard wherein is buried our dreams of a better world. The world will only be improved one heart at a time. The only way out of our quagmire is to repent of the hopelessness we place on the young and begin to hold them accountable for their future. Yes, crimes must be paid in full and it is best that the prisoner pay as much of his retribution to the actual victim than to society as a whole. But we can't lose sight of the fact that we placed the prisoner in his hell. Some days I really wonder who is in the harshest state, the prisoner or the guard that must lose his sleep to watch over him. We would do better to guard the road to the prison and warn all that come near of the dangers within.

MASLOW'S HIERARCHY OF NEEDS

(Or what I paid thousands in college tuition to learn, but knew before I got there)

Okay. I got serious again, and I hate that. So I decided to counter point the harsh prison piece with a topic sure to ring the memory bells of college students everywhere. And that is the one and only "Maslow's Hierarchy of Needs." Who is Maslow, you ask? Haven't a clue. Some guy that wrote a book about needs I presume. But it was dutiful task of almost every professor to teach me this simple concept over and over until I know it better that my own mother's name. And why was this concept deemed so important that it needed to be taught to the prospective graduate at least forty times prior to graduation. No one knows. I mean really, no one knows. Ask any professor why he teaches Maslow's hypothesis and he will scratch his head and mutter. I tried it more than once and guarantee the result.

The crucial premise of Maslow's theory is that human needs are based on a hierarchy that embarks with the physical, moves on to the emotional, and ends at something he referred to as "self actualization." And what is self-actualization, don't know, haven't a clue? I received just about as many explanations for what it was as there were professors endeavoring to teach it. Some professors made strange allusions to Abraham Lincoln; others just assumed it meant fulfilling your wishes and dreams. If this hierarchy of needs is so important then why doesn't anyone understand it? I will make my first and only attempt at explanation and then never refer to Maslow again, God willing.

Basically the theory (and it is only a theory) is predicated on the idea that needs are fundamental at different times and those needs deemed essential must be met first before higher needs can be met. So in essence we must first eat before we philosophize. I always do. First we are fed, then housed, then loved, then learn to love others, then learn skills, and then reach our highest potential, a sort of modern age nirvana. Purportedly, when a man or woman is self-actualized they are being "all that he can be" to quote the Army who stole the idea from poor Maslow for which he received nary a dime. But then he doesn't need a dime since he has "self actualized" all the way to the bank. After all, six million textbooks can't be wrong.

Of course, as you might have guessed, poor Maslow is a simpleton, because the complexities of the human condition defy such simple explanation. Gandhi starved his way to self-actualization, a direct contradiction of the theory. Buddha likewise. Jesus likewise. The fallacy of the theory is this. Most of the people in the world who have achieved some state of self actualization, or what I perceive self actualization to be since no one has ever explained it properly, have as a rule achieved their great success by eliminating or subjugating one or more of the so called basic needs. Walt Whitman suffered great emotional stifling on his way to writing some of the greatest poetry ever written. Kierkegaard virtually starved, after squandering his wealth, writing his essays on philosophy. Socrates was willing to die for a principle, though death is not one of the needs outlined by Maslow. In short Maslow is a twit.

The human ability to reach for the highest that is in him transcends the physical, the emotional, the social, and the vain attempts of colleges to educate genius. The great men of our world do not sit in the cafeteria making damn sure they are fed, housed, and socialized before they reach for the heights of human understanding. I dare to say that the highest need of the human race at this point in history is to have a greater understanding of our humanity and less theory that teaches us to assume that the poor have no ability to contribute to the world. Under Maslow's concepts, we have all assumed that to be undernourished by some system stifles the creativity and beauty of this life. Bullshit. Genius has always found a means out of the prison of the human body. I hope Maslow is listening wherever he is (I'm pretty sure he is dead) and yanks his books off the college campuses of America. He has taught a generation of students that the privileged life is the only life worth living. I hated Maslow's ideas in school and I hate them now. There is no hierarchy of needs, there are simply human beings struggling to make their way from cradle to grave and a few find hunger in many varieties while others find abundance, though their belly is never full. Goodbye Maslow, I need to eat breakfast, oh I forgot, I was supposed to eat first then write, but what do I know, I can barely spell "self actualization."

SUCCESS

✦

(Or how I made my mother proud though I rob the masses of their bread)

Success in America is the most interesting topic to me personally. We Americans speak of success as if it is the Holy Grail of existence. But what is success? How do we define it? I believe I define it differently than those who are affluent, but then I probably would, as I'm not among them. Almost without exception when an American speaks of somebody who is successful he means somebody who earns a vast sum of money. If we introduce ourselves as an educated teacher, others just nod their heads and say, "isn't that nice." But what they are in reality thinking is, "you stupid twit, you went to nine years of college to make thirty grand a year." I must admit I've thought the exact thing on various occasions. Some people have thought that very thing about me, though I don't teach and only went to six years of college. By American standards I'm not successful, but I am, I've just acquired my treasures through books. These treasures are extremely well hidden. I'm akin to the millionaire farmer who drives a 1963 Chevy truck and dresses in worn coveralls. I appear poor of mind, but have a remarkable bank account of useless knowledge.

Did you know that I can recite the seven wonders of the ancient world? I've held this knowledge in place for that one moment I'll be asked that question on a game show and will wow the audience and my accountant by storming off with a huge stash of money. But that is another day, for now I struggle to be successful. Who doesn't? And success doesn't come easy. Almost every successful man or woman I've known has worked ungodly hours and either died young (leaving a desirable, rich widow), or become emotionally incapacitated due to the lack of a life outside of becoming successful. Success has its price and sometimes that price is all you have. Perhaps it is better to be a little poorer and live longer in order to leave your widow less time to spend all of your money on her new boyfriend, while retired in the Bahamas. I myself plan to die penniless, but not out of choice.

I want to introduce a very unfamiliar concept to America. The concept is the virtue of failure. We should never strive to be successful, but should ever be striving to be a failure, and here is why. What is success but the arrival at a certain plateau? Some, after having achieved this plateau sit contentedly by the view it affords and watch the world go by, smug all the while in his or hers great success. But success is not the goal, for all success once it is achieved no longer motivates. It is failure that motivates us toward perfection or even competence. I learned the alphabet, great, so I should sit smugly by the doorway to the local elementary school and taunt all of the first graders with my superb knowledge of the alphabet. Or perhaps I should move on to greater heights and learn to write sentences, then paragraphs, then perhaps entire books? What if I'd never learned past this first success, where would I be now? In jail of course, because a forty five-year-old man hanging out by an elementary school is likely to cause suspicion.

But I think the point is clear. We look at a successful man and admire him because he has acquired a certain skill that we do not have or have not refined to the same degree. But what of other talents, what is this man lacking, because where ever their has been a vast quantity of time spent in one direction there has been little in any other. So we are all wise and foolish, only in different areas. I know nothing of equestrian expertise, but I am all knowing on the subtle skill of verbal assault. Thus it behooves everyone to begin a program of failure, failure is good and positive. Success is its own reward, but it will not leave you fulfilled if it causes you to pause too long on any one vista. Bill Gates is a successful man, meaning rich, but what of his social skills? He needs to set aside his success and start failing at something tomorrow or else he will die the richest, most discontented, man in America.

Let me show you a perfect example. I graduated from college. This is one of the precious few success stories of my life. I was overcome by joy as a long parade of enthusiast friends and relatives shook my hand and patted me on the back. So I had to turn this colossal success into urgent failure. How did I accomplish this, you ask? Simple, I applied for graduate school. So in the summer, nine months after my college graduation, I crossed the threshold into graduate school where, overwhelmed by the unspeakable loads of bullshit getting rammed down my throat I failed in a measly two terms and I'm now officially a graduate school dropout. No, that sentence doesn't carry the same weight of failure as does say, high school dropout, but it does sound a little more defeating than the phrase college graduate. So I turned my success into failure, but what did I gain from this experience? I gained a sense of humility, which has served me so well I remain humble to this day. Oh God how I am humble.

So you see, the secret is to fail. We have been taught only how to succeed, but success is so bare and self-inflating. Anyone within the sound of my computer needs to begin a complete course of failure at once. When we are failing we are growing. When we pause in our success we are gloating, and that is self-defeating. Seriously, we must continue to fail to promote growth. If nature had paused at its first success in the production of life we would all be bacteria right now. But life moved from failure to failure, capitalizing on each minor success, until it reached the pinnacle of intelligence, the dolphin. I fail every day. I strive for success, yes, but it eludes me. Thus I've become through an endless string of failures a wise man. Wisdom is always gained through suffering so I didn't arrive at this state willingly, but I did gain a grain or two of the gift of Solomon. And Solomon, the wisest man to have ever lived, did what with his wisdom? He married seven hundred wives and changed gods. That, apparently, is wisdom in a nutshell.

TELEVISION

❖

(Or how I put the boob in boob tube)

Ah Television. I come at last to that paradigm of American achievement, the television. We are so taken with this little box that it literally dominates the countryside within our homes. When I enter a home for the first time (and I've entered untold thousands selling services through the years) I can always detect the intelligence level of the inhabitants by the position, bulk and number of the television sets. I own two sets, a small one in the living room and a bit larger one down stairs where it can't be seen except by the invited. I do this as television is only of modest value to me and is used primarily to watch movies and cherished programs. But I've been in homes where they display two or even three jumbo sets scattered throughout the house, one in the living room, one in the family room and one perhaps in the bedroom. Often at least two of these sets are on at any given time. I usually think to myself, this is a stupid waste of money, but the poor inhabitants (only poor in spirit because these sets cost thousands) always look impressed with their selections and make up a commentary about the show on the tube to draw my attention to the wealth thereby displayed. However, they fail to grasp that I've entered the homes of the truly rich and none display such vulgar objects as television sets in open view. Instead they conceal them behind huge wooden encasements or perhaps in theatre rooms with ear deafening sound systems.

In general the size of the television set is in express opposite proportion to the span of the owner's brain. The bigger the set the lighter the head or at least lighter the volume of knowledge encased in the head. It is as if a cosmic balance sheet upholds a direct ratio between the observed and the observer. By this supposition we will one day have television screens the size of the wall of our house, but only possess the mental capacity of a six-month-old child. We'll be unable to track simple plots though they are all the same, which is hero gets in deep do-do and in less than an hour discovers a way out with the aid of a twist in unforeseen circumstances, mostly because the circumstances are logically absurd. I know this theory hints at the folk wisdom of phrenology, but hey that is all I can think of after a night of dismembering reruns.

The best shows by all accounts were in the past. The current crop of shows is always judged inferior to what has preceded it. This was what my parents said in the sixties, though most of their favorite programs were westerns, such as Bonanza, and it is what I said to my children in the eighties, though by and large I only remember inane sitcoms that have aired endlessly to new generations such as Gilligan's Island. But there is nothing new under the sun and all plots are basically recycled by a new generation of writers who think they're the first to have thought of them. The absurdity of television is that it now doesn't reflect society, but creates it. I've spoken to infantile people about an event in my life only to have them recant a similar story that happened to them, but in reality was simply the plot of a long forgotten television show. They are incredulous when I call them on it as if I'm questioning their sanity. And of course I am, because it is insane to fail to be able to distinguish between reality and a television show. Ironically this is almost never the case with movies. I believe this is owing to the movies being so much larger than life. No one has difficulty separating the silver screen for the world. But television comes into our homes when we are mentally napping and steals our thoughts in the night.

I'm old enough to remember when my family purchased its first television set. I was two and a half and the first program I remember watching was Superman. I still remember the thrill of getting a new station, our fourth, giving us three networks and channel 12, an independent channel that garnered ratings by presenting pro wrestling on Saturday nights. The birth of ABC was a milestone in our lives for the choices were now endless. Imagine, we thought, having four choices each night to watch. And what did I watch, mostly cartoons? But I could finally choose between the irascible Captain Shipwreck or the ultra cool Ramblin' Rod. However, I'm not so old as to have watched "Leave It To Beaver" in first run. Even in my long ago time I watched the cuddly Beav in glorious black and white as he stumbled through the pasture patties of life in an eternal youth that shall last a thousand years. Color wouldn't have enhanced the experience one bit.

In fact my family didn't purchase its first color set until 1969. I watched the moon landing in black and white which wasn't shocking because their were no color cameras on board the lunar landing module and the moon, for all its October orange, is a dark dull place, typically shades of gray and darker gray. I remember the high drama that black and white could evoke. I've heard it said that black and white televisions can distinguish more than a thousand shades of gray, but a color set is limited to only a handful of variations of each color. The ominous glare of Perry Mason still haunts me. However, the seventies broadcast the whole television world in glorious color and anyone displaying an old black and white was mocked as backward.

Some say that television brings the family together, some that it rips the family apart. I say that it is harmless unless it is abused, which it is in just about every home in America. It is one thing to watch a program on poverty in America and be compelled to action and quite another to watch five hours of "Wheel Of Fortune" each week. I even acknowledge that watching Oprah on occasion isn't so bad. She does promote books, which often sell very well. (Yes, Oprah, I'm available). So television is harmless then? Of course not, anyone with the ability to get on television is endowed with power that kings of old would covet. Television is the most potent medium of communication ever created. A television star is vastly more famous than a mere movie star though the movie star commands a greater salary. And like most Americans, I preach the gospel of limited television much more than I actually practice it. I still find myself on occasion roving through the backwaters of banal programs in those belated hours when sleep eludes me. I've watched all the episodes of "Gilligan's Island" and "The Brady Bunch" and what is the social value of these shows? I don't know, never will, but for some inane reason we all watch them as if Gilligan were channeling Moses. This is precisely why television frightens me. It is mass hypnosis of a par we can't wholly comprehend.

The movie stars and the radio stars avoided television in its early years. Little did they realize that to have a hit on television is the closest to immortality anyone on earth can ever achieve. So powerful is television, and the characters it creates, that frequently it is impossible for a gifted actor who has skillfully created a memorable character to ever live it down. They are often ruined by the experience and are never seen as anyone other than the character they once so brilliantly portrayed. An excellent example is Henry Winkler. "The Fonz" is so strong a character he has completely overshadowed the rest of Henry's life. All subsequent characters are just seen as "The Fonz" playing Hamlet. I think you get the drift. The character becomes real in a way that astounds me. I've heard it said by many actors that they are called by their character's name on the street. Asked medical advice if they happen to have played a doctor. Legal advice if they once played a lawyer. This is the point at which television turns into a frightening experience. The fine line between illusion and reality is thin enough as is, but television weakens the thread even more. Fortunately, there has appeared on the horizon a logical extension of the artificial world of television; it is called "reality" programming. This device calls for the prodding of otherwise sane, reasonable people into bizarre circumstances while they compete for money, prizes and of course the inevitable immortality. I give you "Survivor" the foremost show of its kind.

I love "Survivor" because it is a show that penetrates profoundly into the human condition and exposes an astounding depth of information about the human species. It highlights both our pettiness and our resilience. I watch each episode with baited breath desperately striving to pick the next evacuee. I'm proud to announce that I picked the final five contestants on "Survivor II" in perfect order of their demise. Tina was a tough call, but I have witnesses. I'd sniffed out Colby's unbridled stupidity on an earlier episode.

And what pray tell does "Survivor" reveal. Mostly that we are, at the core of it, not too bright at selecting our associates. Most of the finalists on the first two shows were those that formed the strongest alliances. Buddying up with a premature evacuee was, without exception, the kiss of death. Richard Hatch selected the incorruptible Rudy. Rudy wouldn't betray him, an obvious guess, but no one else looked as if they understood the importance of this alliance. So in the end Richard "the snake" won, but why? Tina "the descendent of some of the wealthiest inhabitants of Tennessee, but she seemed so poor and innocent" also won, but why? Here are my theories. Richard, first of all, understood that this was a game. The younger set were too caught up in "who liked who" to sit down and scheme how to win the damn game. Richard grasped that to win was to divide and conquer. When his tribe was positioned to vote off a member of the opposite tribe he rallied the troops to expel a leader from that tribe and not the weakling, as when voting out a member of your own tribe. Brilliant. Next he clung closely to Rudy, the true soul among the vipers. Brilliant. And last of all, he got lucky. He was almost voted off on one occasion, but survived. Richard was not a snake, but a clever man. So does this imply the clever always win? Yes, exactly that. The man with the most fortitude, who sees furthermost into the trees shielding the future, prevails in the game of wealth in America. So Richard won, just as it should be. But what about Tina, she was so straightforward and nice, she subsisted in a 1200 square foot house with one bathroom, you would've thought she had just jumped out of the backwoods of Tennessee. This was her most brilliant strategy. Is Tina smarter than she seemed? Hell yes.

She manipulated the gullible Colby into not only voting Keith off the island instead of her, she got him to jump for joy at his tossing aside 900,000 dollars. I proclaim for all time that this was dazzling gamesmanship of the highest order. Tina played the game, the people, and the camera to perfection and may one day be proclaimed the greatest player sometime after "Survivor 40" is deemed the final program in the series. I can't wait for "Survivor 17" it will be a game with all of the first sixteen winners. I predict a woman will win it. They all look so sweet as they stab you in the back.

But to get at the root of the "Survivor" phenomenon it must be stated that it is indeed revealing of human nature and there are lessons to be learned from how our lives play out in the greater game we call "survival." Sometimes bad luck happens to an otherwise worthy opponent, perfect example, Michael, who may have skewed the results of the program due to his unfortunate display of unparalleled stupidity via a flaming fire. Old women have been seen by contestants as a futile encumbrance and quickly disposed of, while older men have been seen as wise, paternal, authentic, and resourceful. Both Rudy and Roger are two of the most beloved players. Madelyn may well play out as the strongest older woman to ever play the game, but she lasted three episodes. In both shows the strongest mind won. And I think it is of little doubt that both parties being in or near their forties was a causative factor as the forties are the last bastion of sanity before the brain cells begin to revolt and die. And what might I say to future players? Beware of whom you know, it may lead to your demise. Shape strong alliances and mold the best tribe. Most of all play to the crowd by promising to donate money to charity and to pay the mortgages of friends. I'd like to see Tina's receipts. I think she outplayed us all.

TRANSPORTATION

✦

(Or how to get from here to there the worst possible way)

Of all the absurdities of American life our penchant toward driving ourselves to and fro in full-size, lumbering, overpriced, gas guzzling cars is perhaps the most absurd. A majority of Americans will hop in the car just to visit a neighbor three doors down. And heaven forbid if we don't own an individual automobile. Sharing is out of the question. Our car is our declaration to the world of status and rank in the socio-economic hierarchy. To drive less car than what one can afford is a reprehensible act, which arouses scorn and ire among our neighbors and families. We should be as deep in debt as is possible when purchasing a car. That is our thinking, but why? Because we have all been made to believe there is an emotional connotation to cars. Cars represent the good life. The life of chasing women (or men) and of exploring, getting out and living, though most SUV's never go off pavement.

I've fallen victim to this advertising blitz on numerous occasions. So have you. Models are displayed in an electrifying color out on an open road, the tires blazing as sunlight streaks off the hubs of the polished chrome. Even though in reality the car will look dirty most of the time. Then a young man or woman is revealed, smiling behind the wheel as he or she glares roguishly at the other schleps who aren't fortunate enough to own the car they have so wisely purchased, disregarding that their payments are now equal to half their income. What we need is a commuter car, what we buy is a dream. A dream that is soon shattered in the first parking lot where a disheveled old man slams his door into yours and your dream gets evaporated in a steam of verbal expletives. Ahhh, but wasn't it beautiful, my car, that first hour that I owned it.

I drive a decent car. It's relatively new, relatively nice. I have power windows, air conditioning, automatic transmission and cloth seats. It gets 32 miles to the gallon, which is a socially responsible rate. I drive quit a bit in my work so I feel I need to be reasonable and just accept that my car is neither the nicest nor the fastest on the road. Yet, each and every day, I sit parked in traffic behind a convertible, a Mercedes, a Jaguar, a Lexus and drool and dream to the point of nausea. I own a responsible car, I drive it responsibly, all of which is incredibly boring. I sit behind the Porsche and dream myself into the drivers seat and wish I were that man or woman hustling down the pavement getting a socially irresponsible ten miles to the gallon, but looking oh so wonderful tucked into the leather seat that sits just inches off the ground.

This is the product of advertising. We are made to feel that our car is a statement of our lifestyle. However, I know a Mercedes owner who is afraid to park his car in a public lot for fear of it getting scratched, therefore he almost always drives his Ford Ranger about town. But at least he owns a piece of the dream and that is what truly matters to him. He can feel all of the excitement of ownership even if he never drives the car. It is enough just to be driving down the road in a nondescript pickup as long as you know the dream sits reposed in your garage, ready in a moment to take you on a journey toward the sun. I sit in my responsible car and think of my wife's car, sitting in the parking lot at her work unused, but oh, it so much nicer than my own. I don't drive it often, not allowed, but when I do I'm transformed into a road king that lords over the lesser engined like an icon over the peasants below. You see, her car is fast, very fast, and it is big, wide and demands attention. All those wonderful things my car will not and cannot offer.

When I drive my wife's car I feel so in control of the road. I can speed up and pass anything that moves. I can inch up on a smaller car and prod it onward. I can decide on a whim to make it to Salem in thirty minutes. I love her car for it makes me feel as if I mattered, which of course I don't, but at least I feel that way as I sit in the leather seats listening to a CD on her 1,500 dollar stereo and pretend for a moment that I own the world. Now tell me, wouldn't you pay extra for all this? Of course you would, and you do. I can only imagine the feel of a Porsche under my legs, I will probably never own one, but it is nice to dream, which the advertisers understand so well. We claim we buy a car for its value, its quality, but who is kidding whom, we buy the things because they make us feel like a million bucks though we will never possess but a fraction of this sum.

This leads me to the problems our predilection toward impractical cars has created. Our roads, especially in larger cities are crowded, very crowded. I sit most of my day in traffic waiting for lights to change, for wrecks to get cleaned up, for grandmas to get out of my way. I wait and I wait. My car supposedly can run at 110 miles per hour, but for the most part it travels at less than fifty because the traffic will not allow it. In Portland, Oregon where I live the transportation department is forever striving to make the roads run better, but they no sooner get a traffic jam corrected than enough new people move into the area to create a different one. We have light rail running both directions, east and west, but most users still drive their cars to the terminals, which solves nothing. The government tries, but fails because it is we, the American public, that is to blame. We insist on impossible transportation then blame the government for not providing quality roads. If we would stop over using them we wouldn't need so much maintenance, but will we stop using them? No, of course not. My car is an extension of myself and I'm not about to cut off my right arm to make more room in my suit. As long as Americans have the right of car ownership they will buy the most improbable vehicles imaginable. This will seal our fate, a fate that is not so rosy as our cheeks on a windy day as we sit behind our convertible looking like a million bucks.

This brings me to the future. I see the future in the hybrid cars that are just beginning to inch their way onto the American scene. They are ugly and expensive, but this will change in time. Honda and Toyota already sell good systems that get somewhere in the neighborhood of sixty miles to the gallon while throwing off less than a quarter of the polluted exhaust as does a regular car. This system will work and I foresee a day when virtually all cars will be a hybrid of some sort. Perhaps in a more distant time we will all run on hydrogen, but for now the hybrid seems to be the wave of the near future. I will own one, someday, when they aren't so ugly. I have a reputation to maintain. I see them here and there as I amble about town. Mostly the environmentally conscious or the social innovators who simply must have everything first and by the cheapskates who long to bypass the fuel pump as often as possible own them. I do not fit into any of these categories as yet. I am perfectly willing to own a hybrid car, when Lexus brings out its model that makes me look like I own the world.

Lastly, I think it is important to note that the greenhouse effect is apparently real. We simply must reevaluate our need for speed in light of this startling fact. If we Americans do not forge the way no one will follow. And since we use up about a third of all the energy consumption of the world we are largely to blame for the higher heat. Greenhouse gases are not a good thing, look at Venus, want to go there? How does 900 degrees sound for the perfect vacation spot? Well Venus was once a lot cooler, let us hope earth remains a great place to live because the alternatives are not so great. It is a known fact that the sun is getting brighter. Our little star is passing through middle age and is slowly increasing in brightness until one day, several billion years from now, it will boil off the oceans of the earth and destroy all life and all memory of life on the planet. That means that half of all the time allotted for life on earth has already passed. If we don't stop the heating of the atmosphere that few billion years will shrink to a few mere decades. How stupid to destroy the world in order to get to work a little faster, and a little classier, than the next guy. But we all drive on, myself included, until the sun one day stops us in our tracks and asks the inevitable question. I wonder if boiled human tastes good?

THE INDIFFERENT

◆

(Or I wish I cared but I don't)

All men are naturally indifferent to matters that don't concern their immediate condition, or at least I believe that to be the case. But you may disagree if it is a matter of indifference to you. I'm indifferent to whether you like this book, you are indifferent to whether I make a living from writing it. We are all indifferent-only on different matters, but we all pray that other men are serious about what we are serious about, but of course we are not. We are all seriously indifferent. We care about hunger if we are hungry, indifferent if we are fed. This is the natural condition of man and only the saints have mastered the art of caring while not being directly affected. Of course we don't care about the saints and are indifferent to the cause of Christianity.

There was a brief time in the 1960's when people pretended to care a great deal, but of course the participants soon cared more about getting stoned than world peace or the end of racism. Soon the world became indifferent to whether people cared or not. After all, nothing ever changed. Apathy soon became hipper than philanthropy. But soon the country became indifferent to apathy, and it was best not to care, better to pretend we had things to do other than save the world. This was the era of recession and punk rock. It is easier not to care when there is less to care about. During the prosperity of the nineties we were too busy earning money to care about the poor. What we cared about the most was that we were not among them. The country became indifferent to poverty, as if it was a communicable disease.

Now some of us are poor again and hate the indifference of the rich to our plight, or at least until we get rich again and are too busy to care.

I've often been indifferent to the bounties our country provides, except when the Democrats are in control of Congress (not really.) I grew up in an era of great political passion, the sixties, and yet my whole generation and I are now the most apathetic to have ever governed this country. I'd like to say what a shame, but the truth is that the change was inevitable. Great passion leads to great disappointment, unless the passionate die young. And many of my cohorts accomplished just that. But I survived the tumultuous era to be buried by a mortgage and kids. I'd love to say that I'm indifferent to my mortgage, but that is foolishness, a house is a thing, men are generally only indifferent to ideas and emotion. True indifference is bred of poor timing, and that is the whole of it. We never know when the stars may shine upon us or when we are to be felled by the axe of history. All a man needs to do to become completely indifferent is to avoid the pain of being wrong. Fortunately, even the lowliest of men are passionate about something even if it is only a sport they themselves cannot play.

A leading cause of indifference, I believe, is puberty. It is the one thing we simply cannot avoid. And once having past that raging river the power of indifference has eaten our soul. Puberty mandates both passion and its inevitable end. When we pass over into adulthood we find that nothing of our passion remains. "The world is still the same after all we've been through," to quote the song. This irritates us, so we turn our anger toward the powers that be and shower them with indifference. At least then, we surmise, we get back a measure of our disappointment that the world has killed our youthful enthusiasm. It is our duty at this point to look toward the young to take up the flag of change, then to sit back and criticize the passion they display. Of course, we reason, the young are foolish and want a different world than the one we so valiantly pursued, so let us crush them. And so the whole sad world of indifference renews itself like an eternal spring of uselessness. It makes me so mad I feel like becoming indifferent to the human race, or rather I'd become indifferent if I weren't already indifferent.

I ask the country this question. What would it take for passion to return to the political landscape and again produce free debate (surely those awful city council meetings don't qualify) and for justice to flow like gravy from a spoon? You answer, why a sex scandal perhaps? Or a congressman caught with his hand in the cookie jar, or a president caught lying (surely this is a false statement as all presidents are elected based on the quality of their lies.) So perhaps it would take economic ruin, this rings true to me. The one thing to which we are certainly not indifferent is our bank account. So prosperity is the root cause of political indifference then? Yes, the one thing we are passionate about is the cause of all other indifference.

So I propose we drive the country to ruin in order to change our society for the better. Then we can listen to a new generation of politicians lie our way back to prosperity. This may seem like an endless cycle, and you are right, but I'm indifferent to the status quo. I'd like to see more passion in our lives even if that passion is misguided. Al least the world would be more interesting for a while. There is nothing more boring than a passionless, prosperous society filled with amusements and early death. Where are the radicals when you need them? Oh, I forgot, they are all too busy playing Nintendo to conquer the world.

So indifference is a disease of the rich and hunger the best motivator for change. But America is not a skinny country, we are overweight and bloated on news, infomercials, and entertainment. I believe it is possible for us to live out our lives in complete indifference so long as we are among the fortunate who have no want of bread. But in the end who will care about our passionless dreams. The future? No. We will be ignored, our descendents, no, they will hate us for our indifference. Then surely God will praise us for our prosperity, no, God is ignoring us because we are indifferent to Him. Religion just isn't high tech enough. So what then is the ultimate fate of an indifferent society? It is to be ignored. But why should we care, we are indifferent to our fate. But is our fate the graveyard of democracy? Do not ask the stars, the universe cares nothing for us, in the end it is indifferent.

POWER IN AMERICA

✦

(Or who runs the farm since the animals never listen)

I t's a great mystery to foreigners, and a good deal of Americans too, just who it is that runs our prosperous country. It seems at first glance that it should be the President, but that is laughable to anyone who has seen this man in action. He rules nothing. Head of the military, you counter? No. I doubt if the President of the United States could properly command a raid on the White House fridge. But he employs some awfully clever folk who can command troops and ships and guns and they apparently take orders from the President, though I wonder if they really care what he thinks since the American public often does not. Besides, the President is too involved in various fundraisers to really get a grip on troop movements in Panama. Abraham Lincoln, to my knowledge, was the last president to take an active role in learning to command troops since he was having a sticky time finding a suitable general to command his over-prepared army. He, by all accounts a highly intelligent man, utterly failed. Presidents are politicians, mostly lawyers who quote Latin with surprising ease, while stumbling over the simplest of cultural dialogue. Command armies, the Constitution says, supreme commander, it also says. Good Lord, I say.

Besides the military, who else controls the reigns of power in America? Well, business of course, whom else. Businesses buy their way into the political process in two fundamental ways. First they hire a slew of lobbyists to wine and dine members of Congress in order to get passed into legislation all manner of ill advised and short sighted bills that usually favor a privileged few. The other method is the simplest, the business interests simply donate huge quantities of money to the various parties and campaigns then sit back and watch their influence rise and fall with the candidate's message. The most intelligent of the businesses hedge their bets by giving money to both sides, in a sort of win-win effect. It usually matters little what the candidates overall agenda is, only what his or her particular stance is on the issues most likely to influence future business transactions. And who can fault the businesses really, it is our laws that allow these atrocities of justice to occur and who made the laws, supposedly we did.

All power is futile and short-lived. We see many men, captains of industry, bastions of intellectual talent and plain ogres who have striven all their life for success and power only to be felled by age, infirmity, or a change in the course of human events. At best even a tyrant can scarce rule for more than a few decades and even that is rare. Presidents barely have time to unpack before they are saddled with the label "lame duck." Prime ministers (due to the whims of parliamentary procedure) often have less time than that. So what, in a democracy, is the best way to garner power? It is to make the most shortsighted change possible in the shortest possible time. Usually these shortsighted policies do irreparable harm. So the policies are fixed by more of the same, ad infinitum. And why do we judge our rulers on their immediate impact, because we are Americans and love the quick buck. So what if future generations will have to solve our problems for us, what else are kids for?

True power in America, I suggest, is imbedded in the middle class. Now I know others will disagree and that is perfectly fine if they choose to display their ignorance, that only makes me look smarter. The middle class is huge. There are a hundred middle class inhabitants for every wealthy American. So why do most of our laws favor the rich and why does the upper five per cent of the country own over half the wealth. Because we no longer make choices based on our own self interest, but watch the ads on television and vote for the best looking, most erudite candidate, even if most of his content is pure drivel. And what does he drivel out? Whatever those who have paid for his campaign wish him to drivel out. Even the rich can no longer win an election without corporate sponsorship, so who runs the ship? I don't and neither do you, though you have been told all of your life that America is a government by the people, for the people, and so on. We are a country owned by the advertisers and sponsors of a ludicrous waste of money and time. And we let it happen without explanation. We get what we pay for, and what we pay for isn't worth what we pay for it.

On any given day the middle class could unite in a holler and close down any tax loophole, any subsidy, or any leak of funds by the military or any other organization. We could build schools, pave roads, and provide clean water and air to any stretch of grass in America, yet we do not. This is a mystery greater than how the Pyramids of Giza were built. What prevents us from uniting on any number of given issues and claiming the throne the founding fathers willed to us? Simple, we don't have enough time because we are too busy paying taxes.

In short, we have been fragmented by the various business interests in America whose main concern is in allowing the middle class the luxury of enough work hours to afford the products that have made the businesses rich enough to influence elections. Not a bad racket if you can stay in the game. So ultimately it must be confessed that we have lost sight of the will to perform any task unless there is a monetary reward. Believe it or not few people actually perform to a high level just because they have pride in themselves. We have pride in what our money buys, not in the accomplishments we achieved to procure the money. It is a rather odd, yet non-endearing quality of American life.

THE STATE OF ROCK AND ROLL

❖

(Or what is that crap you are listening to)

Music is always relative to the listener. There are no absolutes, no formula for cranking out popular hits. If there was someone would have made a few billion by now and retired. The process by which a song goes from the creator's head to the radio then to the ears of the public is as mysterious now as it was at the inception of the radio many decades ago. But one thing is constant, the music of today is inferior to that of yesteryear. We all believe that what we listened to as a teen was the ultimate music and that no greater music can or has been created. I listened to the Beatles, the Doors, the Stones, the Who, the Moody Blues and perhaps a little Black Sabbath. The strange thing is so do my sons. Why? I didn't listen to the music of the late thirties, which is about as distantly removed from my day as the music of my youth is removed from my son's day. I never thought in my wildest dreams they would still find the music of my era rewarding and challenging. I find most of the current music they listen to basic crap, but so did my parents think likewise of my music. They listened to Lawrence Welk and Hank Williams, which in their mind was "real music." I thought what they listened to was also crap. I find strangeness in this development that warrants further inquiry.

Was their something special about the music of the Vietnam era? I think so. What has followed the era of the late sixties and early seventies is a hodgepodge of disharmony. First disco, then punk, then grunge, then rap and so on and on. All of these forms are merely a purpose in search of a cause. It is all well intentioned to promote the emotional state of the creators, but in the end it only serves to display the creators own sense of loss at not having a purpose, or a place in this woebegone world. It is all a lost chord. Now I do like some of today's music, a little Creed perhaps, some Metallica, but little else. I find it lacking a sense of direction, which is perhaps indicative of our society as a whole. So what made the music of my youth so endearing as to still fascinate? I believe it was the polarizing force of the drug culture fueled on by the ongoing atrocity of Vietnam. The music of the sixties and early seventies is imbibed with the emotional force of the antiwar movement and with the revulsion of the young at being slaughtered overseas.

As you listen intently to "The End", an anthem of youthful angst written in a drink-induced stupor by Jim Morrison, you sense the pull of dissolution upon your ear. Morrison was not saying smoke a little pot and protest the war, he was saying "we want the world and we want it now." That scared the living bejesus out of parents everywhere. My parents were no exception. My parents, born and bred in the dust bowl years in Oklahoma, could not understand my desire for this music, nor can they still, but the music of The Doors is still strong enough to pull in each subsequent generation. Jim Morrison is having a very good year, though he is dead and doesn't know it. There is a captivating quality to The Doors music that no one has since been able to capture. Jim Morrison was for real, he wanted change, he wanted souls, and he wanted to die. I have heard the critics who say he couldn't sing for shit and that much of his fire was alcohol induced (so is most of everything) but name me the man who has supplanted him in onstage presence and in staying power with the American public. So he wasn't the greatest poet or singer the world has ever known. He was a stage phenomenon and just for scaring the willies out of my parents I eternally thank him.

Of course we can't discuss rock and roll without a mention of The Beatles. They also scared the bejesus out of my parents, but in a more harmless style. I watched them on Ed Sullivan with quiet amusement, I being all of nine or so. I watched my sister lose control of her senses as she watched the four mop tops swing and sway to the screams of thousands of adoring girls in the audience. That was quite a show, my sister I mean. Initially at least, The Beatles were a girl phenomenon. Guys listened, but did not scream. But The Beatles attracted girls so at least the guys were interested enough so they could carry on a decent conversation, such questions as, is Ringo really as stupid as he looks? You get the picture. But in the subsequent years The Beatles grew in musical prowess and song writing grace and eventually created some of the greatest music ever written. So powerful is the depth of a Lennon-McCartney tune that no one has surpassed them in thirty-five years. Sometimes in this world a duo is formed that is greater than the sum of their parts. Such were the Liverpool duo. I think "Eleanor Rigby," "Let It Be," and "The Long And Winding Road," among the finest songs of all time. Such simplicity, such clarity, where is their equal? But the greatest Beatle tune for sheer craftsmanship is "We Can Work It Out." John Lennon tinkling the harmonium in the background created the most excellent harmonic background. Lennon then supplied the chorus "life is very short and there's no time, for fussing and fighting my friend." Dissect this music and you will see genius.

So what happened to the music that came after this explosive era? Well it sort of sank. The torch was passed to a new generation that simply dropped the ball. The reason for some of this was that rock and roll is protest music at its core. How can you protest with rock and roll when your parents are listening to it also? Attempts have been made to separate the generations, wrap, grunge, etcetera, but the fundamental problem is that all these forms are variations of rock and roll, even rap is still subject to the beat of rock, and I might say imprisoned by hopelessly banal lyrics. So what are kids to do? The future may yet hold many forms of music we haven't thought of yet, but until a paradigm shift takes place in music, as it did at the outset of rock with its electric guitars, we will all be able to sit and listen to some good Beatles tunes and think how lucky we were. I listen to the radio these days and often just wish some of these kids would shut up. But there are a few gems in the dung heap. And I keep a watchful eye for the next Beatles; they can't arrive any too soon. My fondest hope is that they are truly gifted and don't try to change the world by playing polka with a beat. But hey, my parents just might understand where they are coming from.

THE WORKPLACE

♦

(Or which is better, retirement or death)

I confess to reading only one comic strip every day, "Dilbert." I find it incredibly right about the workplace of modern America. I have worked for people even more stupid than the pointy haired boss and that should frighten you all. What we have created in our society is a workplace so devoid of humanity and emotional purpose that most everyone who is forced to work within the confines of four walls is driven over a long enough period of time to a sort of satisfied insanity. That is why I've chosen to work out in the hinterlands and concrete pastures of America. I can't live for long in a four-walled prison, even if the pay is horrible and the girls ugly. What I suspect is that millions of you long to join me.

Work is defined as that effort which is necessary to sustain life and to enjoy the pleasures of the flesh. But mostly we Americans work for toys and weekends. Each week the countdown begins on Monday toward that far land of happiness we call Friday. In the event of a vacation or holiday looming on the horizon we are almost beyond joy. How sad it is that most of us hate what we do. I long to be on the fore-front of some major project, but my connection to the company I work for is merely that of a hired gun. I go out into the world and procure for them new customers and they in turn compensate me accordingly. Not exactly brain surgery, but what is other than brain surgery itself?

When I was young I often had to take whatever jobs were offered. I worked in a retail store, newspapers, and while in college at a nuclear research reactor. And what did I do at a nuclear reactor? I swept the perimeter for contamination potentially dropped by some careless grad student on the floor of one of the many laboratories. Then I would walk around on top of the reactor itself and check the radiation levels. Do you know that reactors glow blue when turned on? Neutrons being released radiate somewhat faster than visible light and the eye translates this phenomenon into the color blue. Odd, but there you have it. It is a beautiful shade of cobalt blue and most of the school kids that came on field trips didn't give a damn about the physics involved, they just liked the color. And how did I get this job, you ask? I begged. Oh and as a side note, I used to check the accuracy of my Geiger counter by placing the wand up to a lantern mantle just like the ones you use for camping, they are laced with Thorium. Happy camping!

The modern workplace is a wasteland of ill-advised functions and hopeless human disintegration. In true mentally clumsy fashion, many of the business minds of the prior generation thought it best to construct jobs around specific tasks so that men might perform with the efficiency of robots. Machines were functional, so men must be made to be functional also. So the thinking went, but that is what we used to call "stinkin' thinkin'." Men are not designed to perform the same function over and over. We were designed to learn, to explore, and to evolve. The needs of the industrial age were never meant to be the patterns for humans. The thought that men are somehow suited to these ends has caused the deaths of countless millions while the profits have been absorbed into the pockets of the rich. America must change into a sophisticated society of educated and worthwhile human beings or we will all be so dehumanized that the country will fall into a shambles. The groundwork for our demise has already been laid. Even the high tech industries still treat the vast majority of their employees as little more than glorified slaves.

The drudgery of our workaday world began when it became necessary for people to begin showing up at the same time and place on consecutive days. In the farming world of yesteryear, the cows and chickens dictated our workday and they were very forgiving of an unorganized farmer. The farmer went about his business efficiently, but at his own pace. At the dawn of the industrial revolution it became necessary, in order to improve the functionality of human labor, to mandate arrival and departure times, lunch breaks and vacations, all unheard of concepts in the vast agricultural wasteland of the past. Now it seemed best to work most laborers until they dropped, then replace them with more until they also dropped. Unfortunately, there came an end to the labor supply and new methods had to be devised. Men now required rest and privileges such as bathroom and lunch accommodations, all of this to the aggravation of the factory owner who saw any need to slack as a terrible waste of money. But in direct defiance of the owner's will, productivity improved. It seemed that rested workers actually produced more goods than those that were half-dead. It is a miracle that this information had to be brought to the attention of the factory owner, and was not just inherently obvious.

The workplace evolved as society evolved and increasingly workers found themselves in tiny cubicles sweating alongside many hundreds of other schlumps. The cubicles were all identical except for a few minor details and frequently name plaques had to be installed on the outside edge in order for the occupants to find their way to their own cubicle, as long as they continued to be employed. This was a further extension of the concept of man as machine. If a machine could tap out bits of data in uniform and boring fashion then so should a man be able to do likewise. But again the age-old problem that men were never designed to that end cropped up and the workplace continued to oppress, though it had evolved from stinking factories to sanitary cubes.

This has led to the absurd work environment of today. Like so many nameless cattle we are prodded into our little cubes to work at our inanely dull jobs to produce paper trails for businesses that transact business by the modern communication highway. Gone are the slave conditions of yesteryear, the brutal overuse of children and the crippling effects of toxic chemicals and unhealthy working conditions.

Today most of us work in clean, sterile environments where any display of openly human behavior, such as flirting is seen as discriminatory or harassment. As long as our eyes are glued firmly to the ground and we ask no questions and seek no increases, then we are allowed to continue our shameful existence in a cubical framed by cloth covered board and work out our lives performing a job we do not fully understand. The cubicle emotionally cripples Americans and this is why we all seek our social and emotional survival outside of the workplace.

What should surprise no one is that this environment of dehumanizing workspace is effective at keeping the forces of creativity at bay. It is all but impossible to bring into the cubicle landscape a fresh or novel idea. If indeed an employee does come up with something worthwhile it is immediately stonewalled by management until it is pounded, forged and submitted to tortures unknown so that it can dutifully be credited as the creation of management, your idea having only of course been the seed of their much grander creation. However, if after implementation, the idea proves out as a stinker, you are immediately given all credit for the idea and flushed down the sewer of life. So all of us stick our noses and heads down and do as little as we possibly can. This is our model of human productivity, sad but true.

I must say that I hate work. When a man says that he loves what he does for a living, he is really saying is he loves that what he does for a living is better than what you do for a living. Give the man a couple million bucks and he quits his job in a heartbeat. There are a few rare exceptions, but I suggest these people do not work, but play, such as baseball players, and of course, gamblers. All other folk work and that is no fun at all. I find work a somewhat unpleasant diversion from true living, which is sitting on the beach in Hawaii with a cool drink in hand. Everything else sucks. But work we must and so we do what is necessary to survive, but generally little more. No one is working for the sheer pleasure of the experience, I believe that would be "self-actualization" which as I have already pointed out is a load of crap.

I'd like to see the cubicles torn down like the cell bars they are and get replaced with artificial worlds of plastic plants and wax flowers, at least that would be a truer environment. Americans have created the driest, dullest workplace the human mind can conceive and we are all the poorer for the experience. Imagine if we unleashed all that human creativity on the world. God knows what we might be able to bring into this dismal orb. A few laughs and a few smiles perhaps, that would be new and different? Imagine in this freer world going to a fast food restaurant and getting helped by an English speaking person who smiles, can count change and fill your order quickly and efficiently. Now I'm not saying this isn't a dream, but it is a beautiful one never-theless. See you in your cube, if I can find you. Oh, and please make sure your name is spelled correctly.

THE RETIRED

◆

(Or life is hard under all this sun)

I thought to write on another subject right here, but this one seemed to flow so naturally from the last I thought a false attempt at continuity might be warranted. Of course I am a self-deluded keyboard clacker, so what do I know? There is nothing so appealing in American society as the concept of retirement. It is the fulfillment of all our hopes and dreams, the grand desire of our working lives, to one day live out our golden years in a sunny, yet quiet piece of the globe, where no one will bother us ever again. But alas, that is the very problem of retirement, no one bothers us. We slip quietly into insignificance and are stacked into the corners of the world to be forgotten like ancient cows put out to pasture. What we truly wish is that we were only stripped of our responsibilities, not our titles. Much like the royalty of old Europe, not a bad system when you think about it.

I plan to retire in sixteen years, seven months and eighteen days, but who's counting. I want to travel the globe and live where the sun shines 360 days a year. (Five days of rain, I figure, is about right.) I hear there is still land available in the Sahara Desert, but the air conditioning bills are a budgeting nightmare. So I'll probably compromise by living in Arizona and traveling only to the civilized parts of the world such as Europe and the Mediterranean, perhaps Africa too if I get up any nerve, which isn't likely when I'm sixty-five. The rest of the time I plan to pursue hobbies such as bowling, writing, reading, museums and zoos. Actually now that I think about it just shoot me now. When I retire I want what all retirees want. I want to do all the things I didn't have the time to do when I worked. I want to travel and lounge, travel some more, lounge some more. However, there is an inherent defect in this reasoning. Some of us don't live long enough to fulfill these dreams, my father was one of them, he lived to be 53. He planned to travel and lounge, maybe fish a little too. He got to do none of these things. So is it wise to always be putting off all of our enjoyments until those golden years when we are too old to enjoy most of them? Probably not, but that is our simple fate for the most part.

There is something inherently foolish in saving ones self for retirement as if what we are doing in any given daily routine is simply not worthy to be called living. I think this is sad and a product of our self-delusion that work is all hell. To live a happy and productive life we must leech into our daily living a bit of the magic of retirement. Perhaps go on that trip to Europe while we are still able to walk. Perhaps sail the Pacific while we can still see. The reasoning here is simple. We might not make it to the land of retirement with all our faculties, then what of all we have saved? I know of a man who retired, purchased a travel trailer, a large rumbling pickup and copious camping gear with the full intention of exploring the world he had never had the time to see. The man injured his hip, couldn't connect the trailer to the pickup and sold them both within months of their purchase. My point is this, live while you live, don't save the best for last. Stop and get some donuts along the way. Life is short, don't make it seem to last forever.

I watch the retired in quiet admiration knowing that they have endured the forty odd years of suffering required at the hands of some insufferable boss in order to enjoy, at one's leisure, a few good years in command of their own lives. How sad that what we look forward to is simply life as it should be lived. But who said life is fair. When we are young we have the strength and energy to accomplish most anything, we could travel the world with a backpack, hike across the Alps, or perhaps sail the Pacific in a twenty-foot sailboat, but alas when we are young we are broke. When we have reached retirement, through years of saving and compounding we have the funds to accomplish any travel we wish, but alas we are old and prefer the comforts of a Holiday Inn to say, camping in the Outback. There should be some sort of travel fund set up by the government to allow young people to travel by borrowing from their future pensions. However, this simply is not the plan of life. We are to be broke when we have strength, rich when we are too tired to explore. It seems life is cruel this way and indeed it is.

But what of these hearty souls who buy a huge RV and sell their home and live on the road for the remainder of their days? Well, I say go for it, but just remember, living out of a bus can get old fast. There are no permanent neighbors, no normalcy and routine other than the routine of the road, which is tiresome. And remember that the price one pays for these mobile hotels would pay for six or seven trips around the world. So travel this way if you must. I will see you from time to time and wave from the poolside of some distant Howard Johnson's. Nevertheless, I believe the retired have earned the right to travel as they wish and to stay at home as they wish. Anyone who has so long endured the rigors of work has earned the right to go as they please. I just wish folks would arrive at this age with a little more tolerance for the rest of us. Just go to a retirement community if you want to see cantankerousness in all its glory, old people who drive two abreast on the streets to prevent anyone from traveling faster than the speed limit. Get a life!

And while I'm thinking about it, I hope to arrive at the ripe old age of sixty-five with a little more on my mind than finding the nearest casino. Too many of our retirees are combing the roads in search of idle amusements. There is so much to be done in this world to alleviate suffering. Retirement is the perfect age in which to indulge our altruistic desires, but alas we sit at the side of a video poker machine in hopes of winning the grand prize, which is more idle time to play more poker. I say take these golden years and make them truly golden. Use your talents for the benefit of mankind. I think you will go to your graves much happier folks, and the world will thank you. I know I do.

THE HANDICAPPED

❖

(Or brother can you spare a place to park)

There is nothing so noble, it would seem, as the care and concern for the unfortunate among us that we have labeled the handicapped. Once a handicap meant the number of golf strokes a man needed to whittle off his score in order to appear the equal of a truly exceptional golfer. Now we refer to handicap as any of a great number of mental or physical anomalies. It is fit and proper that we should give special consideration to these poor souls whose ranks we may one day, through misfortune, be forced to join. I think that some future archeologist will be far more impressed with our handicap facilities, special toilets and chairs, than he will be by the space junk we have left tumbling in space.

But in our zeal to accommodate these people we have created one of the greatest absurdities of the modern world. Everywhere one goes in America five or six unused parking spaces sit unadorned by the front door while we must park half a block away. This is a direct result of the actions of Congress. Somewhere in our not too distant past we passed a bill that allowed special parking privileges to the handicapped. Now in theory this seemed all together noble that our society should foresee the needs of the handicapped and make provisions for them. But somehow their numbers were swollen to unspeakable heights because according to Congress about one-third of all patrons of a given business are alleged to be handicapped. The number of handicapped parking spaces is out of all proportion to the actual number of patrons. But the grand question is why? I think you might be able to guess how this came about. Start by sending to Washington, D.C. several moral cowards. Then give them a task that would require them, if they should resist it, to commit political suicide. There you have the start of one awful session.

Virtually all the members of Congress buckled under to the demands of this bill. No one had the courage or moral fiber to stand up and say, have we gone too far? We went too far, way too far and actually those that suffer the most for all this foolishness are those that are marginally handicapped, but don't qualify for the special parking privileges we afford the more severely disabled. Those poor folks must walk further because they are only partially handicapped. And why shouldn't the able bodied be allowed to use those spaces when they aren't being used by the handicapped. We all use handicapped toilets, and yield the floor when someone of true need attempts to use them, but in the meantime they are there for the benefit of all. I love that our country has taken steps to ensure that all citizens may participate fully in the processes of life. Lord knows I believe this to be a small segment of true greatness in our people. But my God, certainly we should never have left these decisions in the hands of the cowards in Washington. This should have been handled state by state. We have taken our desire to aid to the point of logical absurdity. Even the handicaps are sometimes amazed at the vacant space that surrounds them.

And what happens to the poor soul who parks in one of these forbidden spaces. Why he is towed off or charged an unspeakable amount of money for his error. Now I believe we should have parking spaces for the handicapped and it is proper that those spaces should be near the front door, but why the excessive number? We could have used more sense and accomplished the same thing. So the result of all our attempts at altruism is that we have created a monster from which we cannot escape. To attack the bill and correct our folly would require men with courage and there are none, at least not in Congress. To attack a bill that provides for the welfare of the handicapped would be the same as putting a loaded gun to your head. We are stuck with this absurdity for all of time. Perhaps one day there shall be sufficient numbers of the handicapped to fill all those open spaces, but I doubt it. One day we might cure all disease and there will be no lame among us. What then of all these spaces we created for their use? They will grow weeds and we will stop each day to ponder why in the world they were created. No one will remember. One day a team of archeologists from the year four thousand will dig up the site of an old McDonalds and scratch their collective heads at just what the blue signs and multiple stripes across the front of the opening were for. Many theories will be advanced, but I believe the theory that will win out is this. It will be surmised that the stripes and blue handicapped signs were warnings, that those that enter will likely be crippled.

POLICE STATE

✦

(Or please don't kill me I only took a snickers)

The greatest evil that could befall a free people, according to our founding fathers, was the presence of a strong and militaristic police force. Though all such forces are initially created to protect the innocent they always end up being the method that harms the innocent by their own laws. Thus our absurdity today of a police force from whom we all cower. We all want the cops to arrive in a timely manner when we are threatened with bodily harm, and usually they do, but we all avoid them otherwise as if they carried the plague or had terrible body odor. This should not be, the police should be the friend of the law abiding, but they are not. We see them as the enemy if they are not engaged in our immediate rescue. Why is this? Because they are just as likely to arrest us for nothing as for something, and why is this, because we have endowed them with powers they should not have. No police officer in a free society should be allowed to look as if he just stepped off the battlefield. This creates, not diminishes, the risk of harm. Yes, I'm aware that they must deal with undesirables, some of whom are violent and armed and for this we need protection, but walk the perimeter of a fair or concert and you will see a paramilitary force that gives you the impression you are only steps away from Bulgaria. This in the land of the free? Free to do what?

Every day I hear of cases where a man or woman is wrongly arrested and strip-searched, fingerprinted and in general treated as if they were the antichrist just because they may look similar to someone who may or may not have committed a crime. Sometimes this is done for the simple purpose of making the accused aware of an overdue traffic ticket. One time I was traveling in the eastern hinterlands of Oregon and was in the process of moving. I was issued a traffic ticket and then moved so the notice of impending court date was never received. One day a sheriff's deputy knocks on my door and the next thing I know I'm handcuffed, mug shot and fingerprinted. In just moments I post the bail and am back on the streets. And this wasn't even my fault. I clearly told the officer at the time that I was moving and what my new address was. He failed to remember this later. I say this is crap and a ludicrous waste of our money. Our resources need to go to fight real crime and not to pad the dawdling of the underemployed.

We laugh at the drug dealer who is smacked down to the ground, frisked then brutally handcuffed, then dragged kicking and screaming into the patrol car. Just desserts, we say. But I tell you that it is not far from police treating drug dealers this way and the police treating you and I this way. Brutality once begun can only be stopped by even greater brutality. We must be on guard against too many policemen and too many laws. The very laws we create soon catch us in our own web. We are all too human to justify the insane number of laws we are expected to obey. Ignorance of the law is no excuse we are told. Well, I say, then what is the excuse of ignorance while passing the law? We can't trust judges, lawyers and the police to patrol the justice zone for us. They are watching the innocent as well as the guilty. And there really are no innocents because no one can live up to all of the laws we enact. Certain sanity must prevail if we are ever to guarantee we are not hung in our own noose. Today's lawyer is sometimes tomorrow's prisoner and today's powerful is sometimes tomorrow's ice cream man.

When a man is employed to correct the actions of others he is first told that he is cleaning the world for the harmless. This quickly gets the conspirator in the frame of mind to arrest, search and seize. It is easy to arrest the murderers, the drug dealers, the child molesters and terribly difficult to muster much sympathy for any of the aforementioned. But soon it is not the rapist he is tracking down, but the petty thief, the vandal, the aiders and abettors of small crimes. Soon after it is jaywalkers, speeders and back talkers. Soon after that it is the limp, the lame, the unable, the Christian, the Jew, the black and the poor. We employ the police to protect us, but they decide which of the multitude of laws receive the most attention. If we do not supervise and stand aware they may take our freedom from under our noses. I was stopped twice on a back road outside of Dallas, Oregon, not for any crime or suspicion of crime, but just because. The first time a sheriff's deputy stopped me for speeding, but my car could not go beyond the speed limit due to extreme age. When I pointed this out to him he nearly arrested me for insolence. Beware the bearer of the badge; he is a monster waiting to hatch.

In a truly just society the police are the servants of the people. They assist, help, rescue, lead to safety and at times arrest the suspicious, but a free society can't spend enough time monitoring these activities. Anytime we allow the law enforcers to act outside of our immediate gaze we invite abuse and intolerance. Many who join the ranks of the police forces of our land do so because they have an emotional drive to exercise power over another, because they feel no such power in their personal lives. Now I know of some exceptions, and by no means are all police officers corrupt and belligerent, but too many of them are a danger to us and we have laid the carpet of our freedom at their feet. If we do not call the police to repentance, one day they will call on us, in the dark shadows of the night.

LAWYERS

❖

(Or how to make a buck while doing irreparable harm)

This will be the easiest section of my book to write. No one likes lawyers, often not even their own spouses. There is a not quite human quality about their presence. I've dined and socialized with a few and for the most part they can be a pleasant enough bunch so long as you do not wrong them. God forbid you should scald one with coffee while serving cake. That will cost you a hundred grand. And the reason for this financial insult is obvious, there are way too many lawyers, too many laws, and too many insurance companies willing to pay exorbitant sums in order to settle suits brought about by lawyers, who are always professing to be after the rights of their clients, but who most often get incredibly rich by doing so. There is conflict of interest here, money and rights don't mix, a lawyer truly after the rights of his client shouldn't charge a dime. To charge straight away implies an obligation on the part of the client to provide a winnable case. Rights give way to dollars, rich convicts go free and the poor get hung.

Every day in America the profits of justice go into the pockets of lawyers who often bring frivolous cases before the judiciary causing great expense to you and me, but just as often they win a case, defending a man with blood on his hands. Lawyers and judges will argue endlessly over points of law, phrases, objections, quibbling over the minute details of the trial all of which serves to cloud the minds of the jury. And the jury itself is not anything but a lot of folks with time on their hands. Justice does not appear in a courtroom, justices do. This is a great lesson to the uninitiated. The court is an entity run by men, and as men they are fallible, prejudiced, impatient and overbearing. We must seek justice in the laws we make, the courtroom is too late for justice, and it has an appetite for judgment only.

Lawyers do perform one important function in our society, however. They take up a great deal of otherwise non-rentable office space. The law that a lawyer regurgitates is simply nothing but a coded language that the uninitiated does not speak. In effect we pay a lawyer to read Greek to us so that we may understand our rights. If the laws were simply written in plain English we would of course have little need for lawyers. Then what of all that office space? And not to mention the law schools that train young minds to babble. Would we have to convert them over to cooking schools? I think so. In short there has never been nor ever shall be a greater or more ludicrous waste of humanity than in the practice of the law. What we need are enlightened legislators. And please, can we stop sending lawyers to Congress they are only making the situation worse. We need farmers, teachers, nurses, salesmen and rocket scientists in Congress, anyone but lawyers. Lawyers speak Greek so they make laws that must be read in Greek. The public has no chance at justice until the lawyers are forced to abdicate the throne.

It can be argued by the non-Greek speaking public that lawyers protect the rights of the innocent and prevent large corporations from squashing the little man. Yes, they do, but they wouldn't have to if we simply had laws that prevented these entities from doing so in the first place. It is because of the failure of Congress to make adequate laws that the legal profession thrives. It is the American public that suffers because the law becomes a commodity for purchase and the rich can buy more justice than the poor. Now I don't mean to denigrate the proud folks who have gone to three years of law school in the hopes of obtaining a better life, but I certainly wish the country had provided a better opportunity for you to be a member of productive society, for just what is it that a lawyer produces. Paper? Yes, and quite a bit of it. There is no product in the law. Lawyers simply expound and expand the interpretations of the law, which Congress through ineptitude has allowed to be passed with enough murky language that companies and citizens are allowed to seek loopholes. If this seems to you a wise use of human resources then I think you had better get on board to Russia where your every bureaucratic need may be orgasmicly met.

There have been great lawyers in our country. Clarence Darrow and Abraham Lincoln to name two. But those were great men independent of the law. It is generally the point of most law students to desire to convey a large income into their life and not justice or equality. Those law students that do not seek the economic opportunity that the profession allows are simply stupid. Why? Because they seek that which cannot be. Justice can only be brought into the world through the enactment of just laws. And I give to you the unalterable fact that lawyers will never bring such laws into existence. Only the pure in heart will bring purity into the world. Just attending law school places the purity of the individual in question because everyone who so enters knows that he is willingly entering a brothel of the mind.

Now I must confess I once aspired to be a lawyer. I took an undergraduate degree in political science with the understanding that it would propel me onward and upward toward a noble profession, but somewhere along the way I woke up to the reality that the law is simply a waste of time. It is merely a means to spend ones life raping money from corporations and individuals while skimming a piece off the top for your self. This is not a great and noble profession. It is money lending in a new disguise. And what did Jesus do to the moneylenders of his day? He kicked their butt, and so should America do likewise.

DISNEYLAND

❖

(Or how a mouse fed Anaheim)

I t is fitting and proper that we should speak of Disneyland in a book about the absurdities of America. It is, as I am writing this, mid July and I am of course just two weeks away from flying my family and myself to Los Angeles, as is everyone. It seems that everyone I know has or is soon to make the pilgrimage to the Holy Land of fun-Disneyland. Now it must be said that Walt Disney was a wonderful man. He brought goodness and cleanliness into the world, but he was decidedly a strange man who had his animated characters play loose and fast with the facts of nature. Such as plants don't grow long roots in search of water as the Disney nature film suggests, they grow long roots because they are successful doing so. Nonetheless, I like Disneyland. I like to think of my life like this, that I live at Disneyland and only vacation back in Oregon the other fifty-one weeks of the year. That seems right.

Now the world into which Disneyland was born is far different than the one to which it now resides. In 1955, the year Disneyland opened its doors to less than favorable reviews, the average family consisted of 2.7 children, two adults who were married and not dating anyone else, and who were also the children's biological parents. And this long before the technical wizardry that now permeates amusement parks amplified the electric bill. There were in Disneyland a number of completely lame rides and exhibits almost all of which were later replaced. I offer you the mine ride, the house of tomorrow, and the submarine ride. All gone and for good reason, they sucked. As Disneyland continues to amp up the rides and the glitz the must-see factor increases proportionately. New rides, new exhibits, remodels of oldies but goodies such as Autopia, all make Disneyland the never completed entity Walt Disney desired. But if you remember the good old days of the fifties and sixties, don't you find it odd that bikers and gang-bangers, teen pot smokers and grown men wearing Goofy hats all inhabit the park on any given day? What! You cry, pot smoking teens in Disneyland. Oh yea, I've seen it with my own eyes and it is a shame that not enough is done about it. If there is one place on earth where we do not need to be high to have fun it is Disneyland.

I once had a long conversation with the head of security at Disneyland. It was after a Saturday night incident where three teens were thrown out of the park for throwing wastebaskets off the Mark Twain into the river. This after another teen had called his girlfriend a "cunt" while in line at the carousel, a ride designed to please four and five year olds. Not exactly the way you remembered it huh. I remarked that the locals were destroying the place because they would come to the park just to hang out with their friends using their annual passes, and that locals were also willing to stand in line for three hours just to ride a new ride thereby leaving the travelers, some of whom would only get one chance in a lifetime to visit the park, a half way experience. I made a strong case. I told him that I spent an average of two thousand dollars at each visit while the rogue teen spends maybe twenty. I was worth a hundred teens. Changes were immediately made. Now I would love to think that I was the cause of this but I know that many others must have voiced the same concerns and I am happy to say that Disneyland is the better for it. They began to block out most Saturday nights from the annual pass and increased undercover security and remodeled Tomorrowland, which did more than anything else to cure the ills. So many rides had closed near Space Mountain that teens were hiding in the dark corners to do drugs.

But its problems aside Disneyland has done a great job of capturing the public's imagination. It seems every child must be taken to Disneyland at least two or three times before they are sixteen and too old to care. Many families spend thousands of dollars on a trip that racks up the expenses in a hot hurry. Try feeding a family of four at the nearest eatery. About thirty bucks, how does that sound? And that's for burgers, fries and drinks, the condiments are of course free. And why do we do this you ask? There are some unique qualities to the place that makes it a wonderful place to go, especially for men who have little outlet for their inner child.

Disneyland is one of the few places that a grown man can put a hat on his head that looks like a dog with huge ear flaps down the sides and he can wear this hat on a kiddy ride such as Dumbo and no one, absolutely no one, says a word to him. Try that at the local legion hall or the corner bar and grill. It is acceptable in Disneyland because it is assumed by most people that you are being a good dad, treating your kids to a wonderful time, but I promise you that I've seen a group of Japanese businessmen with these hats on their heads and not a child within twenty feet. I love it. Men need this acceptance of which they get so little. I've also seen a grown man squeezing Snow White pretty hard, but this was more understandable than the mouse ears he had on his head.

I'm about to see for the first time the all-new California Adventure. It just opened this spring and I have to say the reviews from friends and family have been mixed. I've always been the consummate Disneyland guide so I'm anxious to increase my knowledge of this new park. I'm the absolute master of Disneyland and can ride more rides and see more attractions in a given day that just about anybody, just try me, I'll bury you. Now California Adventure is exactly this-an attempt by Disney to destroy Knott's Berry Farm. Most of the rides in the new park are exact duplicates or near misses of the same rides at Knott's, and Downtown Disney is a shameless attempt at capturing even more dollars out of each pocket than is now the case. We might soon have to buy stock in Disney just to gain admission to the park.

No one can fault Disney for trying to corner the entertainment market in Anaheim. I would if it belonged to me. Besides, no one cares that Bill Gates has cornered the market on operating systems, and they aren't near as much fun. But beyond the money and oddity of folks walking the same street in search of the same amusement there is a deeper meaning to Disneyland. I like to think that the place fills a kind of spiritual void. It is our Mecca, our Holyland in America. We go there to be in touch with the inner America that is generally so transparent we cannot see or touch it. I go to be American, for Disneyland is the ultimate expression of American ideals, from the fireworks on the Fourth of July to the Abraham Lincoln exhibit on Main Street. We enter the gates to find the America that exists only in our dreams. The America we think once existed, but in truth never did and never will.

NOISE

✦

(Or can you please shut that dog up)

As housing space has decreased, meaning closer houses and smaller lots, the power of the individual to make an incredible amount of noise has increased exponentially. From hundred watt stereos for both home and car, to big screen televisions, to portable stereos for blasting the neighbors, to ever larger and more vicious dogs that bark long into the night at their own shadows. Noise has become the bane of modern existence forcing people to ever-farther distances to avoid the ear crunching madness of American life. When was the last time you heard silence? Never? I wake almost every night to some screeching car or barking dog or perhaps a heated conversation between married neighbors. Noise is everywhere and when will it end?

Noise has always been with us. Even out on the farm there was the crowing rooster and the mooing cow. But somehow these natural sounds didn't disturb the psyche the way a four hundred horsepower engine does at midnight just outside your window. We have increased technology to the point that almost everyone has the power to disturb the peace and what has this done to our sense of balance? I suggest that many of us are losing sleep over the noise and are unwilling to own up to the fact that we need to do something about it.

I once lived in an apartment building that stretched across a large parking lot and filled an entire city block with an endless row of apartments stacked three high. I lived on the upper floor to avoid the unnerving noise of having people walk on my head. One night I felt a vibrating in my ears. It was coming from my brass headboard. I rose to investigate. I pounded on several doors at three a.m. and received odd stares of incredulity. Finally, I placed my ear up to the wall and traced the sound to the last apartment on the first floor nearly a hundred feet from my bed. A lady had placed her stereo next to the wall and it was vibrating up the wood. I pounded on the door and never received an answer. I was ignored. This has become our lot. Electricity has made our ability to be rude almost infinite. I finally moved out, but not before I had lost many a night's sleep.

Dogs, however, are the true culprits when it comes to noise. A dog barking non-stop for hours on end has awakened me and even though the owners are home they do nothing to stop the barking. Apparently, they can sleep through the endless hullabaloo. It has often been the case that a neighbor, upon my mentioning it the following day, has been absolutely astounded that others could hear their dog barking although the dog could easily be heard for three city blocks. Perhaps we are rude, but also frightfully stupid as well. As our society gets ever more paranoid and the dogs in our life get ever larger, we get to the absurd state where we have Great Danes living in postage stamp size pens when they have been bred for open farm life. Why do people have these animals only to imprison them behind a wall of chain link? This seems absurd and indeed it is. Dogs were meant to befriend man, not annoy him.

However, noise is found in many forms. There is also the noise of the car. I truly believed that by the dawn of the new millennium we would have silent cars, oh how wrong I was. It is still a rite of passage for many teens to have a car that makes an annoying array of guttural noises. This they perceive as sexually exciting to the female of the species. Of course it only makes the young man look like a fool, but he does not see it. It is, I suppose, the last vestige of the fifties, to get in one's hot rod and dash through the streets challenging other cars to a sort of modified duel. Perhaps we will never lose this need, but perhaps it will become quieter in the future, when our engines burn pure ions. A young man loves to make his presence known and if we ignore the young they speak ever louder. Modern stereos now have the alarming capacity to make a man go deaf in less than two months. It has been said, "if it's too loud, you're too old. Yes I am too old, but I still hear better than my teenage sons. What's that?

DIMINISHING RETURNS

✦

(Or enough is enough is enough)

There are people I know that own in excess of sixteen telephones. No they don't live in a mansion, but a two thousand square foot ranch home. I still remember the day my father had our first phone installed. It seemed such a luxury at the time, but now a house with only one phone is seen as embarrassingly primitive and God forbid if the phones are not portable and touch-tone. I can recall the lovely feel of the dial as it turned back to its original locale. It had a kind of soothing effect that is somehow lost in the digital age where all we hear are the annoying bell tones that play a kind of non-music, music. We have become imminently reachable and that is exactly what I hate.

You see, I love to be unreachable, to be always out of the house, the office, out of reach, out of contact, because most of the telephone conversations I've had in the last twenty years have been incredibly inane. I hold this truth to be self evident-there are only two reasons anyone ever calls a man, to ask for his time or his money. No one, except possibly mom, calls just to chat, to see how you're doing, to ask about the weather. No, they only want your time or your money. I gave up looking forward to the phone ringing, now I cringe and let my kid's answer it while I pretend to be busy. I hate the phone; it is a device for killing the soul. Give me back the good old days when you had to discuss issues in person, then again, maybe that wasn't so great an idea either. When did we become so annoying to each other? Or was it I that became annoying and I just think it's everyone else?

The aforementioned Bill Gates (whose personality has all the vigor of a stagnant pond) once said something profound. It was something only a man worth 50 billion dollars could say and have the air of believability. And what he said was this. A television interviewer had asked him if he felt different now that he was worth tens of billions rather just a meager billion or two. He said that after a point one could only buy a certain quality of goods and services and after that one could only buy more of these, so he didn't feel any different than in the past. This is a general statement of the law of diminishing returns. In other words, after a man has attainted a certain comfort in life his future comforts, though purchased with ever escalating dollars, nonetheless provide him with an ever-decreasing amount of pleasure. Beyond a couple hundred thousand a year very little quality of life can be purchased. We can have newer, more, more often, but not much better. The law of diminishing returns was placed on earth by a benevolent deity in order to keep us from going insane looking at what we cannot, and never shall, possess.

Let us take a case in point. A man goes to the store and purchases a television. This enhances his life and brings the news, programs and entertainment into his home. It is a godsend on long, lonely winter nights. But then he runs into an occasional problem. His wife of thirty years occasionally likes to watch Oprah when his baseball game is on. So he goes back to the store and purchases a second set for the living room to go with the one in the family room. All is well. Then one night his teenage daughter wants to watch MTV on the same day that the baseball game and Oprah are airing at the same time. So he marches back to the store and purchases a third set for his daughter. All is well. But then one day he gets to thinking how nice it would be to have a set out in the garage for those times he is working with his tools, so he takes the one out of the family room, places it in the garage and goes back to the store and purchases a large screen state of the art television. And again, all is well.

Then the poor man reads a book on efficiency and realizes that the time he spends in his bathroom and the time his wife spends in the kitchen could be better utilized if they could watch the news while taking care of business. So he again marches back to the store and purchases two additional sets. Now the house is filled with the ability to watch television. But at what point did his money stop buying more convenience and his television sets become an obstacle to other pursuits for he has now so advanced his ability to watch television that he has little time for exercise, working overtime, making love, and dining out. At what point then was enough, enough. Probably a mathematician might say that after the first two sets the law of diminishing returns robbed his money of its rightful return. Yet we live in a country where people habitually purchase just such foolishness with their money. Some is good, a little more is great, but too much begins to actually decrease the ability to live better. Put the brakes on America. Life is too vast to put all of your money into duplicate items. If there are two drivers in your family you generally do not need a third car for a spare, ditto televisions, VCR's, and telephones. Though these items have become cheap, take your excess and do some real good with it, send it to me.

CONGRESS

✦

(Or take my cowards-please)

The Congress of the United States was once a noble and exemplary organization. It was full of debate and posturing, rivalries and fire. But it is now only a shadow of what it once was, having been watered down by the incessant need for money. In their wisdom the founding fathers decided two years was ample time to serve your country and then a gentleman should return to the farm and plow on to old age. This seemed reasonable at the time. However, over the years the issues that faced Congress became increasingly complex requiring more time to master. This led to the professional Congressmen that we have today. With half of Congress up for reelection each year and the need to be in Congress for as long as possible at an all time high, the Congress has become a business for collecting reelection moneys. Every step a Congressman or woman takes is seen as a shameless plea for money and the sad thing is that more often than not that is exactly what it is. Lost in the fog of dollar bills is the moral courage to stand up and be counted for a cause. Everyone is afraid to take a firm stand that might hinder reelection. Two years is seen as a down payment on a career and not as a career in itself.

The other hindrance to courage is the need to appear as a party man or woman to the leaders of the Democratic or Republican Party and especially the need to appear in support of the president in case future openings occur in cushy, overpaid government jobs. Everyone in short has become a toady. Courage, moral strength and individuality have been laced with cyanide and destroyed. If a man of true courage appeared on the scene today he or she would scare the living hell out of everyone and be discredited by the overzealous press for three unpaid parking tickets more than thirty years old. In short, we have no room left in our new corporate Congress for courage. We have settled for business as usual and let the reelections begin. No sooner does a junior Congressman take his seat than his reelection bid begins and it never really ends until a better-funded upstart has defeated him once and for all. There is precious little time left for the daunting task of running a country. This is all rationalized by the belief that if one is capable of getting reelected often enough he will one day have a leadership position in Congress where he can really make a difference. Of course by the time a person becomes a leader he has mastered the art of toadyism to such a fine degree that he becomes a yes man for the party leaders. If you fill Congress with toadies then select leaders from among them it should honestly come as little surprise that we get cowards in charge of our country. This is self-evident, don't you think?

Perhaps nowhere on earth does perfect government exist and perhaps it never shall exist, but we should make an honest attempt at such government. The culprit is lobbyists who schmooze their way onto the congressional scene, treating Congressmen to lunch, golf and the occasional black tie dinner. Yes, this is immoral and everyone knows it, but the cowards are too afraid to stand up and say so. Why? Because it would hurt their reelection campaign, the very lobbyists represent the self-same money that the Congressman will need to be reelected so that one day he will be able to make a difference. Of course someday never comes and no one ever makes much difference, but it is a wonderful justification for becoming a whore to corporate funds. There is no escape from this conundrum save term limits and the banning of lobbyists and their money. But if you are waiting for this to happen I might suggest the faster paced pastime of watching glaciers recede. It will not happen in a hundred years because there is no one of courage left in the building. Change must come from outside Congress, namely from Main Street America.

It is a grave mistake to pay congressmen a salary that exceeds their expenses. Congress is a place to put only the most trusted of our society and the wisest. I offer to you that anyone who actually needs the hundred or so thousand to live on for a few months while in Congress is not all that wise, at least not with their money. I can hear you now, but that leaves only the rich to serve. No it doesn't, it leaves only the pure. The rich are too busy making money to donate much time to their country. And what is wrong with a Congress filled with the idle and the retired. Are you prejudiced? We send the wrong folks to Congress. I say it clearly here and in all places, if you find a man that truly understands the way Congress works send him to the Arctic immediately. The last thing we need is a man who understands government gibberish.

Perhaps one day the world will come to a crisis and we will need great leadership to emerge in Congress to stay the course of destruction. I hope by then that we have learned our lessons and retreated to a safer haven, a haven filled with the temporary and the involved. If we continue to allow lawyers to make our laws we will all find ourselves in prison, literally and figuratively. Congress was once great and could be great again. I truly hope that one day we will force it to live up to its lofty aspirations. In the meantime I urge everyone to vote his or her current Congressman or woman out of office in the next election. Why? Because you will feel like a million bucks and that is exactly what you will save in taxes over the next thirty years by voting out the scoundrels that have stayed long enough to figure out how to cheat you out of your money. Change is good, remember what does not change does not live.

THE BURDEN OF DEBT

✦

(Or brother can you spare some plastic)

We have become a nation of debtors. It has become so rare in our daily lives to encounter someone living on their current income that many of us could shoot a rifle a mile in four directions and not create a boundary sufficiently large enough to cover a single human being not in debt up to their eyeballs. And how did we get this way? Somebody made it embarrassingly easy. They mailed you a pre-approved application or perhaps even a card you didn't order. You of course are flattered by the prospect that someone considers you a good enough credit risk to send you a pre-approved application. Of course you are not completely pre-approved, if you read the small print (just how do lawyers learn to write so small anyway) you find that certain conditions do apply, but mostly if you send in the application you will be sent a credit card neatly embossed with your name in gold letters, the choice of color here not an accident. You now begin the lifetime of imprisonment you so richly deserve.

At first you are cognizant that you probably don't deserve the credit you have just received (the application said you might be eligible for up to 10,000 dollars, but your card was only approved for four hundred) and you start by making a few modest purchases, which you diligently pay off each month, for awhile that is. Soon, if not sooner than that, an unexpected comes up. Now an unexpected is an event that you knew damn good and well would likely occur, but which you have pretended never would. So up it comes. The transmission goes out on your car and 1300.00 dollars later you are saddled with a bill you can't pay in full. So you charge it. Lucky for you your diligence in paying on time has earned you a credit increase of three thousand dollars for which they only charged you 49.00 dollars to perform. So you charge the repair and vow to pay it off in the shortest possible time, and so you begin. Four months later, after making four 65.00 payments, you have paid the balance down to 1297.00 dollars, at this rate you quickly realize you will pay off the debt sometime between retirement and death. So you become numb to the monthly bill because you simply cannot bear to look at it each month and feel so powerless over your life.

Then an incredibly interesting thing happens. You become numb to the bill itself, it becomes a part of your lifestyle, you know it is coming so you set aside money to pay it and you take solace in the fact that you are building up an excellent credit rating. Then you go out and charge something you really don't need. Why? Because after so many months you realize that you can put an additional two or three hundred on your card and the payment will still be 65.00 dollars just like before. Since you have already become adjusted to the 65.00 dollars it no longer appears to you as a debt but as a bill, like the water or electric bill. Soon you find that you have maxed your credit limit and this time no more credit is forthcoming. But help arrives just in the nick of time. Fresh from your mailbox a new pre-approved application arrives and the process repeats itself over and over again until one day someone calls and asks you why you haven't paid your bill this month. You answer that there has been a slowdown at work and you aren't getting the hours you used to, but no one wants to hear this so they send you to collections where they destroy your credit forever, or ten years, whichever comes first. Bankruptcy. Once a horrible word filled with allusions to Dickens and poor farms, but now a rite of passage for many middle-agers. I would like to suggest that life doesn't get good until after the first bankruptcy and divorce, however, others might disagree.

Now I ask you who is getting rich, who is really living the good life that is so wonderfully portrayed in the ads for Visa and MasterCard?

You know damn well that it is the credit card companies and not consumers. I reason that anyone who spends the better part of his adult life in debt to the tune of 15,000 dollars will probably pay enough interest to have made him a multi-millionaire if he had invested the payments in stocks and bonds. Debt is poverty, unless an asset backs it. Never borrow money to pay for something that disappears soon after, because that is exactly what happens to your life after the fun of spending the initial credit limit is gone. If you really want to be in prison that bad just rob a bank, hell you might just get away with it and live in Mexico for the rest of your life. Maybe you will get caught and spend twenty years in San Quentin, but your odds are better of getting rich by doing something stupid than they are by using credit cards. So stop it right now.

Accumulating money so that the interest you earn begins to work for you and not your personal labor creates wealth. You let others borrow your money or sink it into assets and let time turn your money into a small fortune. This is such a simple process that it is amazing more people don't take advantage of it. It is so easy in America to try to keep up appearances, to have rich toys like your neighbors, but what most of us don't understand is that most of our neighbors live in absolute terror of an economic downturn. Almost 90 per cent of American households are less than ninety days from financial ruin. Don't you think this might be a little stressful? I do. Get out of debt, stay out of debt, and preach the gospel of no debt to your children. It is the nearest thing to scripture that I actually believe in. Cheers to your portfolio and I hope when you toss your credit cards they thump a banker in the head

TEENAGERS

✦

(Or what is the definition of absurdity)

Can anything be more absurd than the years of a person's life between the ages of thirteen and nineteen, the teen years as they are so frighteningly called? I've raised four teenagers and it seems I am raising them still though most have passed quietly into their twenties. It is true that this is a difficult time in anyone's life. I recall my own struggles to find myself amid the vast array of humanity. I am still at it twenty-six years later. However, children grow up faster and faster all the time. Though I was a pot smoking hippie as a teen, I hadn't even been in rehab until I was sixteen, talk about innocent. I didn't lose my virginity until fifteen, practically an old man. Today it is not uncommon for a youth to be exposed to hard drugs in grade school or to experiment with sex by the age of thirteen. Life is exposing young people to harsh realities long before they are emotionally prepared for the lifelong consequences of their actions. Though a year may seem like an eternity to a teen it is nothing to a forty-year-old.

I've contended with my own children that teenagers only see the surface of things and the deeper interconnectedness of life is lost on their "see it, want it" mentality. I've been proven right more often than not, as my kids have slowly learned as they have gotten older and realized dad wasn't the idiot they assumed after all. Mark Twain once commented, after returning from a trip to the tropics when he was nineteen years old, that he was amazed at how much his father had learned. I certainly thought my parents were idiots when I was a teenager, my children thought I was too. This despite my futile attempts to enlighten them on many occasions. I couldn't see how "cool" something was, as they could, but I knew they simply couldn't understand how stupid what they thought so cool actually was. Yes Madonna had a certain charm, but have you seen her lately? And really how many forms of cancer has she cured?

My children are fond of pointing out my shortcomings while all the while blatantly disregarding their own. I suppose this phenomenon is at its all time peak when in the teen years. My shoes were never sleek enough, my sandals too old fashioned, my shirts lacking in pizzazz, my clothes too dowdy and plain. Yet all this while, as the criticism poured down upon my head, I thought I was pretty cool. How is that for a relative perception? I pointed out over and over again how at their age I was also the epitome of cool and that the definition of cool is ever changing and that to rely on the judgment of others is to deny yourself your own personal expression which leads to ultimate happiness. They of course looked back at me in disbelief. Here in my few words I had successfully proved how stupid I truly was by an appeal to history. That is an argument you can never win, in the short run. Only when the weight of history has poured down upon the teen's head can they see that the here and now is in many ways only a recycling of the past and that they will be supplanted in their coolness by their own children who will mercilessly mock them.

Let me take you back to the year 1971 and describe for you a typical wardrobe for the typical pot smoking teen and see if you don't agree with me that I was indeed cool. Let's start with shoes. As you know Nike was only a fledgling company back in those days and produced only one shoe that I can remember buying and that was the waffle-stomper. It was a tennis type shoe with what looked like a flattened waffle patty made out of rubber-stamped onto the sole. Now these early Nikes were not all that cool because the best athletes in America had not as yet endorsed them. But they were okay and a shrewd mind could see that they had potential. But the shoe of choice at the time was clearly the Adidas three-striped tennis shoe. They were cool and

Adidas had been around in Europe for eons. European items in the early seventies were greatly sought after, though now they are generally ignored.

In addition to the tennis shoe the desert boot was in vogue along with a few forms of leather boots not related to cowboy boots. Cowboy boots were uncool to the greatest possible extreme. Also, a complete wardrobe would have included a wide leather belt and a wide leather wristband for your watch. All this leather made some people smell like a cow barn, but that was pretty close to the effect all hoped to achieve. You see, we were getting back to nature, whatever that meant. For pants there was of course the beloved Levi button fly 501's. It took an eternity to unbutton your pants just to take a simple pee, but they were rugged, lasted forever and relatively cheap, less than ten bucks. For shirts it was required that they have vertical stripes. I had several of these shirts though I never truly understood what the appeal was of the stripes. For socks we wore white ankle highs with again, a stripe or two at the top. This was the base outfit for any styling, happening dude, but there were some slight variations.

I must mention the bell-bottom pant and cords, as they were called. These were updates of earlier renditions of teen attire, but they worked well to round out the ensembles of the guys. I had about five pairs of pants, two pairs of jeans, two pairs of cords and one pair of bell-bottoms, this was a typical ensemble. Now I defy you to say I wasn't cool. I was, I was. Now my children stare at the pictures in my high school annual and laugh themselves sick. All of the guys had long hair, or at least long by today's standards and the whole look of tie-dye and bell-bottoms seems absurd. I relentlessly point out to them that their children will one-day laugh at their tongue piercing and belly button rings and also laugh themselves sick. They look at me with deep concern, as if I might actually have slipped into a state of early senility and they state plainly that nothing could ever be cooler than piercing. I disagree, but who knows for certain what the future holds. I look forward to watching their children look back at their old annuals and I will smile the smile of the wise. My children will discern in a burst of insight that the old man wasn't so dumb, as they had supposed.

CUSTOMER SERVICE

✦

(Or how to count change, though the register tells you how much it is)

While I'm on the subject of teens I thought about my latest experience at a variety store. Most of the counter help we meet today is under the age of twenty so it is a barometer of the state of the high school education system to order a few meals at a local burger joint or to stop at the local department store. I do this on occasion though I hate the service. I guess the price is right and at least there is a store on almost every street corner. Recently I went into a store and picked up some film that I'd left the day before. This came to a total of $3.47. I handed the young lady a five-dollar bill and awaited my change. I expected $1.53, but I was handed instead a ten a five and a one and about eighteen cents in change. Now I can appreciate the occasional error in my favor, but I knew this poor young girl was liable to have to stay an extra hour just to balance the till, so I pointed out to her that she had given me too much change. She looked at me with large doe eyes and said, "How much should it have been?" I replied that the correct change was $1.53 and she looked again at me with large doe eyes. She said, "You must be really smart?" I pointed out to her that the very machine that accepts the money also displays the amount of change to be given back. This came as a complete revelation to her. She again looked at me with large doe eyes and said, "Thanks sir, I hadn't noticed that."

Now you are all saying okay, but she was the dumbest bear in the woods. Think again. On the same visit I purchased a few more items and checked out at the front register. The total came to $6.50. This was a no-brainer. I handed the girl a ten expecting $3.50 in change. Not only would the register display the correct amount, but it would only require the picking up of two quarters along with the three one dollar bills. The girl, a cute young blonde, handed me one dollar and fourteen cents in change. Now I was mystified. It is one thing to pick up the incorrect amount of paper bills, but how does one screw up the fifty cents part? I asked her, "How did you come up with fourteen cents when the total was clearly fifty cents?" She replied, "Cause that's the right amount." I asked her to please give me the other two ones that were due me and she immediately blurted into the intercom and paged a manager. Thank God I thought, at least now I'll be dealing with someone who can count to a hundred. Think again. The manager looked over the receipt and asked me what the problem was. I replied that I'd given the girl a ten-dollar bill and not received the correct change. She informed me that they would have to wait until the end of the day to see if the till balanced to find out if indeed I'd been shorted. As you might well guess the till balanced perfectly.

Now I hear you saying okay, so he went to the dumbest place on earth and got the worst service imaginable. Think again. The service at the department store is actually considered not too bad when compared to the average experience at any of the local burger joints within a mile of my home. I live in a big city so there are about ten burger joints near my house and I do frequent them, though again, I'm at a loss as to why. I have yet in two years of living in this neighborhood been spoken to or waited on by an "English is my first language" attendee. Many speak Spanish, a few Cantonese and a few French, but no one in particular speaks English with any degree of proficiency. So you are saying to yourself okay, but the cash register is so sophisticated now that all they have to do is press a few buttons and the order pretty much makes itself. Then the register tells them how much change to give. Yes that is true, all they have to do is press little buttons, but I've seen young people turn this into a frighteningly protracted extravaganza. I once waited for forty-five minutes just to place an order. No I didn't wait in a long line all this time. I was alone in the line. The person waiting on me was working his second order, period. He had been set up to work alone. He didn't speak a word of English and I speak no Spanish other than "Bano," which I've been led to believe means "bathroom."

By an act of divine intervention I was blessed with undue patience that day and repeated my order sixteen times without raising my voice. I truly felt sorry for the young man who probably needed the money to help his family, so I wasn't looking to yell for a manager. He couldn't find the right buttons on the screen and all this because I wished to substitute a shake for a drink. This was simply too complex a task for the stillborn and he flustered and flushed as the order proceeded. I tried everything, including hand gestures. At one point I walked behind the counter and placed my hand on the very meal I wished to purchase and then pointed helplessly to a picture of a shake. Finally in order to get out while I was still young I changed to a soft drink and the young man smiled so wide I felt as if I'd just freed him from slavery. Again you are saying okay, the guy was new. But I guarantee you this wasn't the worst service I've ever received. Once I was unfortunate enough to be waited on by a young man who began, for unknown reasons, to count the quantity of fries in my fry box. If you understand his reasoning please send me a letter with the full explanation. I know it will be good.

So in our society of increased productivity and vast economic increase why do we get such lousy service most of the time? Well, the reason is simple, because we are cheapskates. The reason a burger joint can put a meal in your mouth for less that four bucks is that they have to pay next to nothing in wages. You and I refuse to work there so they are left with the bottom of the barrel. It is our own fault, not the fault of the stores. If you go into a nice mall store where suits sell for a thousand dollars I assure you the service will be excellent. You will pay about a hundred per cent mark up for the privilege, but the suit seller will be able to count change. So the next time you enter a store and feel a moron has just waited on you remember that you wanted it that way, to save a few bucks. Cheapskate.

IN THE BEGINNING

*

(Or my dinosaur is bigger than your metaphor)

There is always a storm brewing in some far distant corner of our country pertaining to the teaching of evolution. The beginning of the world is measured by many to be the sacred province of the Bible. I've read the Bible and don't recall it stating anyplace that the world was created 6,000 years ago. It takes, I believe, a profound leap of imaginative faith to suppose the world was created only 6,000 years ago. After all, we have trees that are almost half that age and trees are a relative newcomer to the world, as is man. But if you believe the world was created yesterday or on any other day you may wish to ponder, I say fine. But don't teach it as fact in our schools, because it is your opinion only, you have no proof, no theory, no evidence to back your claim, so I say remain silent on the subject.

I do not believe the theory of evolution in any way refutes a divine origin for our universe. There is no need for an appeal to scripture to circumvent the product that is our world. It surely at times seems divine enough to me, though it is crammed with distinctly non-divine creatures on its surface. But the fact remains that evolution is indeed a scientific theory backed by mountains of evidence, backed by radiocarbon dating and by the fact that we are here and thriving on a planet that required hundreds of millions of years to manufacture the oil we run our cars on. All this does not suggest that our creation didn't have a purpose. I presume there will always be those who discredit the idea that we are somehow descended from the apes, but here's a question for you.

If we suppose that the universe was created by a divine entity then it must have been created out of a love for what would subsequently follow. The universe began as a hot ball of fire less than the width of a single proton. It might be simpler to say the universe was simply one thing, one creation and as all things were contained in the fireball so are all things in the universe today just aspects of the same origin. Does this not make everything in the universe divine if the beginning were also divine? I think it does. Therefore we can state that all things are the offspring of divinity and the product of the love required to create such a universe. Therefore the matter that forms the molecules that process our blood and the very cells of our brain and the brains of all living things had as their origin a divine providence. So it is easy to assume that whether our superior brains evolved from the ape or were formed full-blown from the mind of God it is the same either way. We are divine and nothing less.

The problems come when we must decide what to instruct our children in school. Many people believe that the teaching of evolution diminishes our roles as Christians, but I do not agree. The entirety of the universe is divine or at least has a purpose that we might readily believe is divine, for even science must agree that a spiritual element is hardwired into the human brain. It is there, and is the source scientists believe of mystical thought and teaching. Why a spiritual element if it attains to nothing?

There is no absolute time, so what is a year? A year on earth isn't the same as a year on Mars or a year on a massive planet surrounding some as yet undiscovered sun. So when someone says the universe was created in 6,000 years what do they mean? If one reads the story of Genesis, the word day appears in the book before there is a world to measure it by, so what does the word day mean? I think it means "period." Or in other words, an epoch in which certain profound changes have occurred. For example, the "day" the first stars were formed, the "day" the first planets cooled, the "day" the first life forms clung to the sides of volcanic rock. All of these "days" are as real as the rotation of the earth, which in reality is only one small interpretation of the word day.

I believe as science moves forward genetics will be able to retrace the entire evolutionary trail of the human species. What then of the literal translations of the Bible? I think it will spur a revolution in thinking about our origins and the place of religion in our world. Does the fact that man evolved make it any less necessary to live by the principles of Jesus? Think for a moment about what he said, and I am here only considering the man as a member of his times and neglecting for the moment the unanswerable question as to his divinity. The man said things like "love your neighbor as yourself," "do unto others as you would have them do unto you." Does the fact of our having evolved as species over billions of years diminish in any way the power of these words? Of course not, they are eternal and timeless. We have pigeon-holed ourselves into too narrow a definition of religion and it is a shame because the Bible I think teaches many wonderful things to our young people. Things I believe that are of benefit to humanity. But when these great principles are cloaked in hysteria the young turn their heads in shame. They forsake the message because of the tone of the messenger. Because we first teach them something that surely cannot be true they assume that all of the rest of it must also be untrue. That is a travesty.

I believe in balance in life and I believe it is within the realm of necessity for our youth to be taught that other explanations also exist, but these explanations must be clothed in the evidence. The evidence for divine creation in 6,000 years is none. It is only a belief of faith and nothing more, so teach that as truth for it is truth. It is my hope that in the near future the world will allow the tolerance of evolution in our thinking for there is far too much evidence for its truth than can ever be proven completely wrong. We must incorporate the idea of billions of years of process into our religion and our life if we are ever to get at the deeper and more profound mystery of our existence, for that is the method by which to live a happy and abundant life.

THE HIGH COST OF DEATH

❖

(Or please don't die, I can't afford it)

It would seem to a sane and reasonable person that the day one ceases to eat and breathe would be the last day it would cost money for you to live on earth. After all, it should cost little or nothing to only lie there and decay, unless you factor in a small cleaning fee. However, it costs the average person about five to ten thousand dollars to be properly buried and placed in a small rectangular piece of land reserved for this very purpose. The why of this escapes me. Who says that a casket should cost thousands or a plot of land hundreds? And really, who needs acres of fresh flowers when they only die in a few days. Couldn't this all be cheaper and allow the poor the dignity of not impoverishing their offspring even further? Of course it could, but it doesn't. The question is why?

I believe the why of the high cost of death is simple. By passing a few well-meaning laws it became necessary to have a professional handle your remains. This professional needs to charge a fee. Now he could simply obtain the body and burn it, then drive it home in a cardboard box, but this will never do. You see, there needs to be a funeral so the unlucky survivors can take a long last look at the body though the body in the casket has little relationship in appearance to the actual living person. The body is caked with layers of bad makeup and then dressed in a suit the living person would never have had the audacity to wear. So this leaves us with an absurdity we have little ability to fix.

Why? Because it involves the emotional state of a person who has just lost a loved one and you don't mess with those folks unless you yourself have a death wish.

Bit by bit, over a few decades, a simple body preparation and a pine box evolved into a highly lucrative profession. The funeral home business is alive and kicking although its customers are not. And how was this done? By a horde of morticians who used the sympathy of widows to raise the bar on the cost of a funeral. First it was flowers. They were relatively cheap, often being plucked from a nearby garden at little cost. Then the casket grew progressively more ornate. First a few fancy handles, then a bit better wood, then a little extra craftsmanship, until you reach today when for twenty grand you can be placed in a box that is far better built than any of the furniture you owned while alive. Absurd? Yep.

As a professional salesman I know a good sales job when I see it. I once had the misfortune of arranging my own father's funeral. Now luckily the local mortician happened to be someone I knew from school, so I wasn't sold the usual bill of goods, but it was fascinating how the process of casket buying took place. Now understand that my father was cremated so the need for a casket was nonexistent. I was forced to purchase one because of a relative who was traveling from Arizona to Oregon for the funeral (though she'd never visited the deceased while he was alive in twenty years) and who had expressed great sorrow that she wouldn't be able to see the deceased one last time. I pointed out to her that the deceased had been flattened by a fallen tree, but she was inconsolable. So off I went to the casket store to shop for a soon to be rotting box that would cost me a years pay.

And just where does one shop for a casket? At the funeral home. Most, if not all, of the modern day funeral homes have a special room set up for the display of quite a few caskets starting with the lowest price godforsaken piece of crap to the ultra luxurious specially padded vault so the deceased will rest comfortably throughout eternity. Now of course when you look at the casket you are being visually manipulated into transferring human emotions onto a dead piece of flesh, but you do get caught up in the emotion more than you realize. I say this now and for all of time, the dead just don't give a shit. The whole package, the casket, the flowers, the music, the fancy limos, all of it is purely for the purpose of consoling the living into believing they have properly cared for the deceased. All so they can raise their head in society and claim how much they loved the dearly departed. It is all a load of crap sold to the vulnerable public by the greatest salesmen in our society, funeral home directors. He or she is an unparalleled master in coaxing money out of your pocket. Lawyers could take lessons from morticians. The director's somber face is not due to his touching sympathy for your recent loss, it's due to the bill he just received for the repair of his new Porsche.

This is how the buying process took place. I, as I've mentioned, had little need for a casket in the first place, but I knew I had to fabricate something so I was determined that I'd buy as low a priced casket as was offered just to console my aunt. I did try, but ultimately failed. Here is why. I was led into a large, darkly paneled room where before me in staunch rows lay the variety of caskets the home offered for sale. Now it was pointed out to me that it was unethical for them to pressure me into the purchase of any particular casket so they would leave me alone to decide for myself. That is one of the biggest lies I've ever been told. The room itself was a veritable smorgasbord of salesmanship. I was most definitely not alone in the room. The spirit of salesmen past haunted my every step.

I walked gingerly toward the first casket (now I point out that casket buying isn't like buying a new car, you are attempting to purchase something you wish you didn't need) it leapt out at me from the table and sported a decent price tag of only a few hundred dollars. Sold, I said to myself. But then I peered at the plain wood box and realized I could never place my father in such a thing. Why? Do you think he cared one way or the other, hardly? I cared, I cared about what people would think of me for having positioned my own father in such a horrible casket. The casket, the cheap one, looked like the furniture you often find at Goodwill. It had the look of extended use by a band of gypsies. The handles were cheap plastic squares. The wood didn't match top to bottom. The varnish was uneven and looked like it had been painted backwards by a dyslexic. The stand it was placed on looked like varnished cardboard and the whole box looked like it might not last the day. It was going to be burned to a crisp anyway, but I couldn't buy it.

I ambled up each row noticing that the price tags grew progressively better engraved and longer. The few hundred bucks of a couple of rows back had become the few thousand of "everlasting memory" as the most expensive one was called. But it was nice. It would have made a wonderful sofa with a little retooling and some nice upholstering. I gasped at the thought of spending my entire inheritance on a useless box so I thought and thought and arrived at a compromise. And it worked. I bought the second to cheapest casket available and then for seventy five bucks bought a huge flower bouquet that rested so abundantly on the top as to hide the fact that it had cost less than five hundred dollars. Perfect. The whole thing was burned into cinder and deposited into a tiny lot costing one quarter of a full square and I got the whole thing done, with taste, for two grand. My funeral director hates me to this day.

THE LOTTERY

❖

(Or how to become a millionaire without really trying)

I've always wished to stop into a convenience store one day, purchase a lotto ticket, win, go straight home, call my boss and quit my job. Millions of others have the same fantasy, but I'm afraid that is all it is, a fantasy. Why? Because the odds of winning are about the same as being struck by lightening while exploring caves and the greater the prize money the greater the awareness. As the dollar signs twirl ever higher the lines grow ever longer until it becomes all but impossible to purchase a soda. But as the number of players increases the odds diminish. Sometimes these odds reach into the hundreds of millions yet still we play. All in the hope of one day being able to pick up the phone and telling our boss where to stick his lousy job.

I'm too conservative with money to play the big lotteries that fly past now and then. I play only the scratch off tickets that at best have a payout of a thousand dollars. Not nearly enough money to quit one's job, but enough to provide a week or so of happiness. But most people bore easily of the small time payoff and graduate to mega lotteries run by the state, sometimes by several states at the same time. It is a phenomenon and a mystery. For the average person betting ten bucks a week over forty years they could simply invest that money in a good mutual fund and retire the millionaire they seek to be, but that involves something we Americans hate, saving. It is so much more fun to take our chances in the game of life, to roll the dice and hope for sevens. But we never win; it is all a huge waste of money. The precious few that do win, and understand that these people are more rare than the famous few, often squander their new fortunes in a matter of years. Great wealth must be accompanied by great discipline. The fact that you play the lottery instead of investing is a pretty fair example of your lack of the necessary goods to cling to your money in the extremely unlikely event that you win a little.

My son is fond of pointing out that we once came within minutes of winning a million dollars. We were near Washington Square Mall searching for a place to eat on the very day that a man won the million-dollar prize in McDonald's Monopoly Game. We selected another McDonalds a mile away due to a lack of parking. He has never let me live it down. In his mind we were inches, moments, nanoseconds from being rich. I've pointed out to him numerous times that a particular McDonalds serves hundreds if not thousands of people a day and that our odds of being the one lucky customer were no better at that location than another, but he doesn't get it. We were inches from winning he tells me still, inches. I suppose this is always the reasoning behind our continued play. We know someone who knows someone who once won a few grand in the lottery or in this or that game. But the world is so small now that within three phone calls anyone in the United States can be located. So everyone knows a friend of friend of a friend who won big. But that doesn't mean we will ever win. For most of us the lottery is only an amusement and a vehicle for fantasy. I might suggest a good book instead, but that would be met with incredulity.

I remember during my wasted years, the ones I spent suffering in college, taking a class from a professor that was spearheading the drive to get the lottery started in Oregon. Now Oregon is an eccentric and quirky state. We have no sales tax, no self-serve gasoline stations and ultra high property taxes. So it seemed to me that the lottery had little or no chance given that everything in Oregon is voted on by petition or referendum. I was positive that a state that had resoundingly defeated a sale tax ten times would unquestionably forbid the lottery, which had been shown in other states to rob the poor, promote domestic abuse, and to foster the establishment of gambling anonymous groups. But oh how wrong I was.

Oregon sunk knee deep into lotto mania and has never returned. Convenience stores in Oregon are little more than lotto headquarters that sell pop and beer to customers waiting in line for the next big game. In addition, in our wisdom, we established several Native American casinos that are now sprinkled throughout the state as if someone had tossed pins at a map and decided to locate a casino wherever a pin landed. Some are near major cities and some are so far out into the desert they would be buried if a thundering dust storm happened by. Now I'm all for giving the Native American his due, which is a chance at a decent education and a good life, but do they really need to profit from our stupidity in order to gain economic equality. Yes, exactly that. The foundation of America is self-interest. Let the Native American send his child off to college on our losses at the wheel. Let him win back the money he lost on the land that was taken from him. It serves us right. I've read that the interest on the twenty-four dollars we paid for Manhattan would now be worth ten trillion dollars if it had been invested at a modest interest rate. Too bad the locals didn't have a good bank. But now they have even more powerful medicine, a roulette wheel and a deck of cards. I suggest learning to deal in case the Native Americans choose in the future to hire the economically disadvantaged.

THE ELECTORAL COLLEGE

*

(Or how George Bush stole America)

O kay. This is the most exciting section for me personally. Finally, after sixteen years, I will put to use my political science degree. It has been a long, fruitless wait, but the time is here. I majored in political science for no apparent reason. I think it sounded better than sociology or home economics or animal husbandry. I had some vague notions about law school, but deep in the crevasses of my mind I knew I'd never go because there was simply no way to graduate law school without actually studying. However, it was and is possible to graduate college without studying too much and I accomplished the feat in a mere five years when it should have only taken four. But despite the fact that I passed six courses in which I never purchased the necessary textbooks, I managed to learn a thing or two about politics in America.

The first thing I learned was this, don't rock the boat. This is the first law of politics in America. We hate boat rockers and typically toss them into the dustbin of history soon enough. But this I confess is a late addition to our convoluted manner of business. It took about a hundred years for us to hogtie the political process so that boat rockers couldn't get elected. Abraham Lincoln was a boat rocker who was elected because he ran as a Republican against two Democrats, that is the simplest way to explain why we have a two party system today. It was quite obvious to everyone that two against one wasn't fair. We also took note that the election of this backwoods boat rocker caused the country to split in two and affected the subsequent deaths of six million people. America took an extreme dislike for boat rockers after that and have elected precious few since.

The second thing I learned was that the two party system wasn't in existence because people only had two points of view. It exists because the two points of view didn't like other points of view getting in their way. So they passed enough laws, restrictions, rules and regulations to make it all but impossible for a third party to capture enough votes to win even a local election. So today you see only the occasional Green Party candidate sprinkled here and there on an occasional ballot. This candidate never amasses much more than a tiny percent of the vote and functions more to irritate the two major candidates than anything else.

The reason for this party of two is directly reflected back onto the Electoral College, which initially served to dissuade one region from dominating another, but now serves almost the sole purpose of keeping the two major parties in power. You see, with the Electoral College it is an all or nothing proposition. You win a state or you don't. Whether by a million votes or one it is the same. So a third party candidate can receive a sizeable chunk of the votes, as Wallace did in 1968, and receive absolutely no electoral votes. Thus you see no great rush to change the antiquated system by Congress even though the system allowed a man into the White House who doesn't belong there.

All in all the system has served a purpose. What it does is prevent the country from being so divided that the person garnering the highest percentage of votes has only a small minority of voters in his or her pocket. This is what happens in Europe all the time. In Italy a few dozen political parties toss out a few dozen candidates and each receives about ten per cent of the vote, or less. If a party garners much more than that it is elected the majority party and given the daunting task of forming a ruling party although less than twenty per cent of the voters strongly back this shoddy government. So in steps the coalition. Several parties from the not too left or not too right of the ruling party are invited to join in the fun and form a majority party that rules with all the ironclad strength of a wet rag. At the smallest provocation a vote of no confidence is called and the government crumbles like a house of cards. Although this may have served Italy well it has not made them an economic world power. The Electoral College is the strongest reason why you do not see this sort of coalition in America. In our system one party wins. Period. If it has a minority of voters so be it. Thus ruling is made possible as the party has at least a small consensus. So the question remains does the Electoral College still have a purpose in American life?

The short answer is this-yes. The Electoral College serves to bewilder and confuse almost everyone every four years. Long into the past are the reasons for its creation. Regionalism has very little sway on the public consciousness. The Internet, along with job-hopping executives, has diluted our once regionally defined country. All Americans are from nowhere and everywhere. We need to abolish the Electoral College in order to breathe new life back into the political landscape. Its deletion would bring about a desire for change and a chance for new ideas to grow and blossom. Now that I think about it that is exactly why it scares the hell out of politicians. It makes the future harder to control. But that is why I love the freedom of our country, we were never meant to get old and stodgy, but to be forever young.

DIALING FOR DOLLARS

※

(Or don't hang up, I've been on hold since yesterday)

One of the supreme blessings of living in a technologically advanced country is the joy of calling up one your local utilities, communications providers or credit card companies and asking to speak to a representative. Frankly, I'd rather spend all of eternity in a hot burning hell than speak one more time to most of them. I've spent a record two hours forty five minutes on hold to one phone service provider in order to cancel the phone due to poor customer service. They had the audacity to ask me why I was canceling. Perhaps I could come over to your house tonight and skewer your buttocks with a red-hot poker, I thought. I'm canceling because I can't seem to speak to someone who is not an idiot. Even still they persisted with trying to prevent me from canceling by offering me a month of free service. What service, I asked? There was no service that is why I'm canceling. Hold on please, was the reply, I need to get a supervisor. I got a supervisor who was only a tad more literate than the first person and he proceeded to give me two months of free service both of which I declined. But why? He asked. Because of poor service, I replied. Oh, he responded. I think at last he finally got the conundrum we all live under. You can't get good service so you cancel, but it is hard to cancel because you can't get good service. I call it catch one-two because I don't believe most of these customer service reps can count to three.

Of course the feistiest component of any customer service conversation is the dialing itself. No, you can't just call up and speak to a living creature. First you must wade through a bewildering array of options. Some of which are bizarre if you don't understand what is being asked. The first option of course is, do you wish to speak in Spanish or English? Having passed this first obstacle (I always wonder how the Spanish speaking understand the English speaking person when he asks if they want to speak in Spanish) it is now necessary to move on. The next question might be something to the effect of, press one for billing information, press two if you need to change your personal information. Then the torture continues, press three if you need to speak to a customer service representative, press four if you would like to add to your existing service, press five if you wish to cancel your service. Do not, I repeat, do not press number five unless you have just gone to the bathroom and are equipped to spend at least an hour on the phone. These places aren't quick in the first place, but extra sluggish to take your order for cancellation. I suggest a plate of finger food at the ready.

Lest you surmise that I don't know what I'm talking about let me assure you that my daughter works in one of these god forsaken hell holes while she struggles to muddle her way through college and bum a few bucks from me for gas. Now what I'm about to tell you is the gospel truth so take notes. Even though you have already given these companies every piece of personal information at your disposal at sign up they always ask you to repeat it when you call in. Now you may be guessing that they need this info in order to more rapidly reply to your needs and that is absolute crap. What they are doing in almost every case is stalling. By the time your inquiry reaches the correct person this person has absolutely no idea what information you have divulged to the party of the first part. None. They have been wasting your time in order to fill dead space while the right person is freed up to respond to your call. Kind of makes a man want to hurt someone doesn't it?

My eldest daughter (a master at dealing with customer service centers. Okay, let us call them what they really are-customer abuse centers or since my company's call center is in Texas I refer to ours as not a call center, but a y'all center) recently attempted to purchase a pair of tennis shoes from a mail order company, of course they sent the wrong size then charged her debit card twice causing her account to go into the negative. She was upset to say the least. She called the service center and chewed on a ladies ear for an hour or so. Problem fixed, right? Wrong. They sent the shoes again and they sent the right size, but sent two pairs and a new bill even though she had been charged twice for the first pair. After a great deal of ear chewing and swearing she got the charges reversed and now has two pairs of shoes and three credits to her account. So all in all she ordered one pair of shoes for sixty dollars and received two pairs of shoes and one hundred and twenty dollars in credits to her account. A small profit yes, but worth the trouble? So there you have it, the primary cause of bankruptcy in America. Too little money going into the bottom end of the business, yet companies never learn.

One day I called a customer service center for my bank and actually spoke to an English-speaking woman who seemed to know just what to ask and when to ask it. I almost cried. We had the loveliest conversation and she thanked me for calling and asked if she could help me with anything else. I was so impressed with this lady I asked for her supervisors name so I could personally call and tell them what a great employee they had and how much I appreciated the level of service at the bank. She replied, why thank you, I am the supervisor, in fact I'm the president of the bank. I understood immediately, we ask for too much from minimum wage workers, if they could actually help us in the first place they would have real jobs. My daughter reminds me that it is quite common in her center for the reps to routinely ignore a customer's question, no matter how many times it is asked, and then at the end of the conversation ask if there is anything else they can do. No, you should say, I think you have destroyed the last vestige of hope I once held in humanity, good day.

CHILD SUPPORT

❖

(Or how the courts stab without a knife)

I'm unusually qualified to speak on the subject of child support because I am one of the rare men who has both paid and received it. When I was paying child support I felt I was treated like crap by the state enforcing agency out to stick fathers, even those who paid their full amount. But later, when I was receiving support, I felt I was also treated like crap by the enforcing agency so I at last got that it was just the agency's way of dealing with everyone, which I found oddly comforting. Child support is the conglomerated concept of the American legal system for the fair and equitable support of children. There is however, nothing fair and equitable about it. Although states spend millions in enforcing support they spend nothing on visitation rights. Do you see an inherent prejudice against men here? I do. The state lawmakers that have given us child support as the solution to our societal ills have left out a few necessary details, such as when should support cease.

In my state, Oregon, a parent must pay child support until a child is eighteen and not attending school. If the child decides to attend college the support may be extended to the age of twenty-one. There is only one little problem. Two parent households are not required to pay one dime to their children past the age of eighteen. No parent is required by law to pay for college except those who have had the misfortune to divorce and who are in all likelihood the least able to afford it. Prejudice? In the extreme. Now I advocate the aid of children through college, though not to the tune of full rides, but according to my state I'm responsible for providing for a child who may well be living off campus with a girlfriend or boyfriend and make more money than I do. This is absurd.

A father who claimed it was morally reprehensible to force child support to continue past high school sued not long ago in Oregon. Now it was fairly reported in the states largest paper that married parents are under no obligation to support children past the age of eighteen and the end of high school. The state won the case and the judiciary claimed it a great day for Oregon's children. But it was a sad day for the Constitution. College is an option for young people not a right of birth. I would rather believe I lived in a world where parents would willingly help their children to achieve their goals and to give financial assistance where possible, than to live in a world where such behavior is only inflicted upon a chosen few. And I'm well aware that many women pay child support as well, so this issue is not restricted to men.

The reason for all this absurdity is the fact that fathers make easy societal targets. They have been seen in the past as mere wallets with little or no rights beyond the providing of greenbacks. Attempt to collect child support and the state will leap into activity on your behalf, attempt to claim visitation rights and you must hire a high priced lawyer and sink thousands into debt to get your due. And why? Because in the past almost all of those paying child support were men and they were regarded as the ones whose financial situation improved after divorce. Partially true I admit, in the past at least. If you doubt that these laws were enacted to extract a toll on men just try talking to any woman you know who is paying support and ask her is she thinks the system is fair. Most, I believe, will answer that they understand the frustrations men have been struggling with much better now that they are on the inside looking out.

Now lest I am misunderstood I want to make it clear that parents most definitely are financially responsible for their children until the age of eighteen or until the end of high school. That is a parent's duty.

And if you are required to pay support by all means you must pay it. I paid to the last dime I owed and that is that. What I am strongly opposed to and think absurd is the enforcement of support beyond the age of eighteen and the end of high school because two parent families are not under the same obligation. This is clearly unfair. Yes, I believe parents should continue to aid their children past that age, but wouldn't it promote a greater bond between parent and child if that money were given out of love and not necessity. I believe with all of my heart, with all of my conviction and belief in the general goodness of the human heart that if we removed the requirement from the laws to support a child in college that, on the average, most students would receive more money not less than they now receive. Many parents are financially able to give many thousands of dollars more to their kids, but do not because the legal obligation to pay support angers them to the point they refuse to give one dollar more than is required.

How then do we go about changing the laws? We probably don't. Understand that it is not the primary goal of most legislators to help the people they represent but to get reelected. The surest way not to get reelected, they believe, is to support a controversial law, especially one that involves a change in child support, which most legislators hold as sacrosanct. Again, we elect cowards for the most part and get what we deserve. I hold out little hope that this law will change in our state. Child support is still viewed as a duty men are to perform for the children they create. And are men responsible for the children they make? Absolutely, but the court needs to get out of the parenting business when that child has reached an age where it can conceivably, though not often, earn more money than the parent who is supporting them. In our high tech area, there many twenty-year-olds out-earning their parents, yet if they decide to take a few classes on the side, the parent is required to pay support. Logically absurd.

BEANIE BABIES AND
OTHER COLLECTIBLES

✦

(Or how to go insane without really trying)

I suppose I could have written this section using any of a number of collectibles; sport cards, sports memorabilia, lunch box collections, Star Trek paraphernalia, or any number of others. I picked beanie babies because my daughter used to run a candy store that sold them and has told me priceless stories about the types of people who purchase them. I think these stories represent the whole collecting culture rather well. I collect nothing so I must admit that my first hand experience here is a bit limited. I will, however, struggle to make some sense of the whole phenomenon if I can.

I spent many happy years clueless to the whole Beanie world. I'd actually never even heard of them until one day I went to visit my daughter in the mall and otherwise polite looking individuals were stampeding her usually quiet store. A long line snaked out of the front door and drifted coil-like around a far corner. She looked harried as she passed out slips of paper to the people in line. When she finally had a moment she approached me and I couldn't wait to find out what was going on. Free giveaway, I thought, perhaps a drawing for merchandise or even cash? Nope, totally dead wrong. I was informed that the line was a line up for the right to purchase, at full price, the new beanie babies that had just arrived that morning. Full price, I asked incredulously, no discount? No, full price, she answered. And this line snakes clear around the outside of the building? Yep, at least two hundred folks in line, she replied. Full price, I asked again? She then rolled her eyes. Full price, she stammered. Okay, I thought, where do I invest in these creations? Oh, and by the way, just what are they? They're little beanbags made to look like animals and things, she replied. Let me see one, I asked?

I clasped a small, fragile glob of carpet-like material filled halfway with a substance I couldn't name, but seemed to be made of toxic waste or something to that effect. The critter had the appearance of a bear though it was out of proportion to any bear I'd actually seen. It was cute. Something I might like to win at a carnival perhaps. I might even be persuaded to buy one or two of them for Christmas for a buck or two. I asked how much they cost. Six bucks, she replied. I looked intently at the doll. I reasoned that there was perhaps fifty cents worth of waste material on the outside and truly doubted that the inside stuffing was anything but free discard from a nuclear waste facility. I blurted, good markup I bet. Yep, she replied. Someone, I reasoned, was making a killing here and too bad it wasn't me. But the deep and abiding mystery that presented itself was why did people want them so badly? I first thought it was one of those female deals, but the line contained many men and children. I needed time to think.

Several years later I had the pleasure to be working a fair for a security company while being positioned next to a lady selling these beanies, as they are called. She told me the reason they were so popular is that once a particular beanie is no longer made they become valuable; some of hers that looked no different from the others were worth up to three hundred dollars. I gasped. They were nothing but old quilts stuffed full of god knew what. I was dumbfounded but at least I'd made a discovery as to what was behind all the hoopla. Beanies made money like a stock held in hopes of market resurgence. I understood that. But as the days wore on and as crowds of people lined up to buy ever more beanies I came to realize that most of these people were not collectors at all, they just thought they were cute. The collectors would eventually make money off these same folks. Fair enough.

The true hard core fan and collector will stoop to next to nothing to get the latest beanie or to get an opportunity to purchase a particularly hard to find one. I want to add just as an aside that the stories I am about to tell you are true. It will be hard to believe that humans can do these things, but I assure you they do. Consider yourself sufficiently warned. For several days prior to a shipment of new beanies my daughter would lather the crowd, so to speak, by announcing to only three or four souls that the beanies would be available for purchase at 7am on a particular day. On that particular day about a hundred or so hardy souls would we waiting in line outside the store even though she had told only a small handful about the arrival. The beanie word had stormed through beanie culture with the power of a brushfire and now hungry, tired collectors and fans awaited the arrival of the appointed hour.

My daughter stands only five-one and about a hundred pounds, but during these beanie moments she held the power of a god. Six foot six inch men cowered at her presence for fear that one faintly wrong word or turn of phrase might eliminate them from consideration for the choicest beanies. She would paste on the window a list of rules that needed to be abided in order to receive a blind draw of one beanie. A blind draw means you get what you get and don't whine. Anyone breaking the rules would be excused to go home. If the natives grew restless my daughter would step out, point to the rules and dead silence soon followed.

At the appointed hour the first arrivals would be let in to a special area to receive their beanies. The first lady in line on most occasions was a wheelchair bound woman who arrived each time around 5am when the security guards opened the mall up to walkers. This woman would spend her extra hours praying, literally, for a good beanie. If she got what she wanted she praised God, if not she assumed she had committed some terrible sin so as not to be worthy of a really good beanie. She would then pray to be better. Some consulted Taro cards, others chanted; a few crossed their fingers when their time arrived. Some were happy to the point of tears when a choice beanie would appear from the back, others cried when a dud appeared, but they religiously followed the rules so as not to eliminate their options in the future. However, the all time winner was a man and his two-year-old boy. Remember I said this was true.

One of the rules (aimed at thwarting unscrupulous mothers who would bring even babies to the drawing) required that to receive a beanie it must be asked for by the person in line. This prevented some mothers from bringing in five kids and leaving with six beanies. If the kid could talk and ask for a beanie they received one providing they also paid for it themselves which with kids always required cash. One man, I'll call him Stupid, brought in a toddler who could hardly talk. He placed the kid on the counter and stuffed a ten-dollar bill in his hand and asked the kid to tell the nice lady what he wanted. The kid said nothing; he just sat and stared. The man glared at the kid focusing his eyes straight ahead and asked the kid again to tell the nice lady what he wanted. Nothing, came the reply. The dad shook the child right there. Red blood flushing the man's cheeks he asked again, this time with clenched teeth, tell the nice lady what you want. The kid said nothing and began to cry. The dad, now furious, got down to the child's level and slapped the poor kid. Finally, through tears, the kid said, beanie. My daughter got him one and the two left although I'm sure the poor kid got a royal beating when he got home. Nice harmless hobby, you say. Since when are humans harmless?

HABITAT

✦

(Or get lost and don't come back)

O nce we humans take possession of a place we are hell bent to never give it back. Whether that territory is claimed from Native Americans or from the wild creatures that used our land for trails long before men ever walked on this continent. What is ours is ours. By the way my stepdaughter who is five feet-nine, a hundred and twenty five pounds with pretty brown eyes suggested this section. Unfortunately, she has a predilection toward dating young men with no jobs or who live with their parents. If you have a job, live independently, are under the age of twenty-five, don't smoke, chew or use tobacco, don't use drugs, have no criminal record, don't find twelve year old girls "attractive" then e-mail me. Perhaps we can arrange a meeting.

The conflict of space is an old one, dating back to the first cases of overpopulation. In the pre-human era species existed in a state of symbiosis. Each species filled its niche as best it could and those species that didn't cope well with this arrangement went extinct. Sometimes species coevolved with the one species allowing the other to progress, such as in the case of bees and flowers. Everywhere one looks in the forest, the meadow, and the desert, a distinct intertwining of life exists. Fleas live on the backs of cattle or dogs. Bacteria allow plant eaters to digest their food. Animals live in trees, which themselves give cover for the growing of fungus, it is all a deep intertwining of existence the way it was planned from the beginning. Then along comes man and destroys the game plan.

Man wants all of the land for himself and doesn't want to share. The first thing man does is mow down the trees to make way for the super-highways. Then he mows down a few more trees for side streets then plows up a few hundred acres of prime farmland for a shopping mall. None of this space is shared with the abundant life that surrounds it. Go into the nearest mall and holler when you see your first deer or snow leopard. You see, we don't leave a space for the little creatures to live. They have no choice but to move out or die. However, their off-spring don't understand the why of this and sometimes return to old haunts just for kicks. And what do we do then? We call animal control and shoo them away or recapture them and take them back to the wil-derness where they belong. If there are animals in the city limits they are pets, dogs and cats that generally do little of anything except eat and poop. Living things were meant to live near and with other living things.

I worked for years in the pest control business. I used to sell pest control to homeowners who wanted to kill every crawling thing within a few hundred feet of their house. Some people were even deathly afraid of spiders and wanted to never see another one as long as they lived. It was their preference that all bugs, no matter how harmless be killed at the nearest possible convenience. I usually obliged as long as the necessary dollars were forthcoming, but I can't say that I always agreed with this philosophy. Many insects do good things to our world. That is more than I can say about some humans.

This desire of ours to kill every living thing in our environment is absurd. We often do not realize the symbiotic relationship with these insects and our outer world until it is too late to change course. We must learn to accept that nature intended for living things to work in harmony. Even we humans need bacteria in our colon to live. Donne said, "No man is an island." I say that no man is even a separate soul. We are an amalgamation of living organisms that work together to pro-duce the "I" of consciousness. This is how the world interconnects in its natural state. To cleanse our world of all the life that should be in it is to cut off the soul from the very life force that sustains it. Have you ever wondered why zoos are so popular? Children love the zoo because in their innocent state they know that we should live among the animals. It is rare today for a child to grow up anywhere near a farm, kids in New York often can't tell you where milk comes from. Sad.

But the animals keep coming back. They have an inherent need to use the same trails that their ancestors have used for thousands, if not millions, of years. I live near a place known as Fanno Creek, which is little more than a meandering ditch that wanders through the urban sprawl of Tigard, Oregon. Though during the day the trail that accompanies the creek is filled with walkers and joggers it is not uncommon at various times of the year for a few coyotes to be seen wandering. This causes panic among the residents, but the fact is that the coyotes have been using Fanno Creek for thousands of years and only recently has it become a jogging path for yuppies. We need to realize that the world was not created in a vacuum, but in a whirling of life forces and that we need as humans to accept the nature around us and try not to shield ourselves from what is ultimately for our benefit. If we do not learn to surround ourselves with life we will ultimately live alone, or not at all.

In the past farms were small affairs, each a few hundred acres consisting of several fields known affectionately as the north forty, the south forty and so on. In between these fields there were fences and these fences had small rows of grass and shrubs that grew along their bottoms. This small strip of nature housed hundreds of small creatures that thrived in the protection afforded them by the ground cover. As agribusiness has taken over the small farm and turned them into mega ventures the rows have given way to endless pastures of thousand acre plots with nothing as far as the eye can see but unadulterated farmland basking in rows of grain. Unfortunately, the little critters that used to live in the strips of grass have all had to move on to find shelter or indeed have been killed in the process. We simply, as human beings, must stop destroying the places for habitat in our world. We do not fully comprehend the magnitude of our stupidity, or at least we will not understand until it is too late. There is no quick buck worth the end of the balance of nature. I hope you are listening and watching a squirrel out your window as you read.

WEDDINGS

❖

(Or how to go broke before getting started)

I 'm not sure who thought of the idea of an elaborate wedding. A marriage should be a simple affair involving, at most, the couple, a few family and friends, and a minister or other legal authority. But I've been to a few weddings that have cost upwards of ten thousand dollars and these weddings were modest compared to others I've read about. Unfortunately, in most cases about a year or two down the road, when cash has been crunched, the couple is seen to lament their foolish extravagance wishing instead to have saved a few dollars for emergencies. This revelation seems to only come in hindsight. Try reasoning money with a soon to be bride and see how far you get thrown.

I suppose that it all started with a wealthy man who threw a lavish party for his newly wedded daughter and all the neighbors soon after were trying to keep up with the Jones'. Weddings must now include music, from a hired singer, flowers arranged by professional florists, professional photographers (how can we ever trust so important an event to Uncle Harry?) to take endless pictures only two of which you will ever display in your house, a church or other facility to house the two hundred guests you have invited though you would be hard pressed to name the half of them, and of course special clothing such as wedding gowns, tuxedoes, maid of honor dresses and the like, all coming to a grand total of half your net worth. And what do you get for all of this money? Well, I'm not really sure because most of the time the couple gets too drunk at the reception to remember much.

I do enjoy weddings, especially ones were dinner is served afterwards at an expensive hotel. But the truth of it is the money would be of far better use if placed in a stock portfolio and allowed to rest comfortably for about forty years. The new young couple would of course retire millionaires if they skipped the elaborate wedding, but like I said don't use reason to make this point too strongly with the bride to be. Most will argue that it is the parents who mostly foot the bill and often that is right. But wouldn't it make more sense to set the youngsters up with a nice gift of invested cash rather than treating all your friends to a free meal at the local Holiday Inn? Do I really need another round of free champagne cocktails and finger food or does the young couple need a down payment on a modest home. You see it is not our ability to earn that keeps us poor but our disability in not seeing the outcome of our actions. Even the poor become rich if they wise up. But alas, the wisdom often comes later in life when it is too late.

Does this mean that a wedding should not be a wonderful, emotionally charged event? Of course not. It is a day of celebration and should be shared with family and friends followed by a short honeymoon, but we have blown this event out of all proportion to its actual importance. The true wedding takes place many years later when the young couple has become older and realizes that they are no longer two souls but one. That is when the true celebration should begin. By all means, bake a cake, take some pictures, have Cousin Sarah sing a duet with her alter ego, whatever brings joy into your life. But please stop bankrupting your future by spending money that is all but wasted on fruitless dinners, and professionals. Even if you can afford it, don't. I know that the wedding industry will try and send assassins my way for my heretical views so I won't be publishing my address with this book.

A wedding should be about the future. It is not so much an event in and of in itself but a promise of a future of happiness. The most absurd way to start this endeavor of happiness is to spend your way into instant poverty on wasteful extravagances. Remember that flowers wilt and die and are ultimately thrown into the trash. The beautiful three tiered cake with the delightful plastic bride and groom on the top is soon excreted into the local sewer. The champagne and beer are soon filling the rivers and streams of America. Photographs get lost, become faded, and are ruined in moving. The only thing that lasts is the memory of whether you had a wonderful experience on your wedding day and if you haven't gone deep into debt there is a good chance that you did.

What reality can every married couple bestow on the young newlyweds? It is that the cause of most fights is over money, or sex, but the fights over sex are due to the tension created by a lack of money that leads to diminished desire. Money is the number one cause of household incivility and the source of the initial tension is the draining of the bank account on the wedding day. Now I understand that there are wealthy people who can spend small fortunes on these events and still provide a nice nest egg for the young couple's future, but really do we need to release a few dozen turtledoves to solemnize the occasion. Use discretion and reason at this event. It will be all the more beautiful for the focus on the emotion rather than on the decorations that soon are carried out with the trash.

OF DOCTORS AND
DENTISTS

✦

(Or how to fleece the public by claiming to
help them)

Now I am the first to admit that there is a serious need for qualified medical personnel in this and every other country. We need bright, educated minds to help cure disease, heal the sick, and repair the lame. What concerns me is the cost of these services and how the professions are to blame for that cost. Does it really need to cost eighty dollars for a doctor to tell you what you already suspect, that your have the flu? Of course not, then why does it cost that much? Because the medical profession, along with the legal profession, have the best unions in the game. That is why. They decide who and how many will get to join in the fun. That is the sole reason for the high cost of primary medical care. The supply of available doctors is diminished while demand stays constant or increases and wallah, you have an increase in price. Simple economics. Charge more than any reasonable person should pay, and if they don't like it send them to Mexico for alternative care.

Now I do not wish to diminish the efforts of the many fine people in the medical trade. After all, many of them are as blind to the economics of the situation as the public is, but there are unscrupulous practitioners and they are all but impossible to root out. Why? Because they have the best union in the game baby. They have a strict, if you are in the game don't kiss and tell policy, and it works like magic.

Short of publicly displayed incompetence or blatant disregard for human life it is impossible to bring a doctor or dentist to the table to account for his or her crimes. They practice on as the public suffers. As I sit here today, writing in my basement, I have just completed a flossing of my teeth. Every time I floss between my two molars on my left side I wince in pain. Why? Because an incompetent dentist drilled a little too erratically and put a small hole in the tooth next to the tooth he was trying to drill. Guess what happened when I complained and demanded he fix the problem. That is right, he billed me for his services even though he had been an incompetent boob. Is there something wrong here? Yep.

If an auto mechanic fixes your car and it breaks down a day later you can take your car back to the shop and in most cases they will repair it for free assuming that the new cause is related to the old cause. But if you should go to a doctor or dentist with the same complaint, that they didn't help the problem you paid them for, they will again bill you for additional time. You see, there is no accountability in the professions. Complain and a surgical steel curtain will crash down and drop on your head like a giant pair of tongs. It is best to simply wash your sorrows in a good beer. I would love to have my tooth fixed, but that would entail having more shots, more pain, more aggravation and I'd rather do my suffering in small doses while I floss, but what a shame we have a dental profession that will not stand behind their work, or repeat it if it is bad or just plain wrong.

Understand one thing perfectly well. Doctors don't know a hell of lot more than you do about the human body. New techniques, new medicines, new methodologies were not invented in your local doctor's office. Research scientists working at various universities throughout America developed them. Local doctors simply are hired to apply these techniques to your body. Often they have only a slightly more appreciable understanding of what is taking place than the patient. I'm not talking about their inane ability to recite even the minutest portion of your body in Latin, but in their ability to understand the human organism as a whole. For the most part doctors are also excellent plumbers and carpenters of flesh. They can hack, tape, prod, snip and sew with the best of them, but ask a doctor exactly how the human body repairs itself and they are stumped. Most have no more clue than a college freshman.

The air that a doctors walks around his office with is just that, an air. It is a game they all play to entice you to believe in them far more than you should. They cringe if ever questioned on any part of their service as if you were asking God to explain His mistake in creating mosquitoes. I am a doctor, they say, how dare you. Well for someone who has spent years studying biology and science I can assure you that I've been treated many times by a person that truly had little idea how to treat me and simply bluffed their way through the exam in hopes that an okie dokie and a slip of paper with archaic scribbling on it would suffice for a sufficient reason to fork over a days pay for the experience. Never, never in this world have any important procedure performed on your body without three opinions, the opinions of two doctors and your own. Your opinion is just about as likely to be correct as the former two.

Doctors and dentists do well when performing a well-tested and oft repeated procedure, such as filling a decayed tooth. But when you get into the deeper areas of human medicine they are usually at a loss to explain. Many, many people have died on this planet due to a misdiagnosis by a trained medical professional who believed wholeheartedly that they were saving the patient's life. The human body, as well as all sophisticated systems, is infinitely complex with subtle interactions and interconnections that are not easily understood. Question anyone who claims to understand the body in all its aspects because I assure you that you are dealing with an idiot. No one understands the inner workings of life, no one. We can fix and repair and occasionally perform an obvious diagnosis, but the actual processes by which this occurs are still a mystery. Remember that once upon a time a woman entered a doctor's office, complained of cramps during pregnancy, and was given medicine by an all-wise, all knowing physician. Several months later she gave birth to a baby with no legs, she had been given Thalidomide.

DIETS

*

(Or you won't stay thin, but you'll fatten a few wallets)

Dieting has become the American obsession. Everywhere you look, in magazines, on television, in stores, you see the various diets and diet strategies advertised. This one really works, they all say. But what about the six hundred diets before this one that said the same thing but in reality didn't work at all, you ask? Well, they were all wrong, they say, this one works. And so you plop down your thirty bucks, go home and await the miracle, which of course never happens because there are no miracles.

We all want to believe a fantasy and the fantasy is this-even though you are fat because you eat too much food, exercise too little and take in a hundred and fifty grams of fat a day you hope and pray that a bottle of pills will come along and cure all of your problems for you. Everyone needs to be paper-thin, all the magazines say so. So we spend and spend in hopes of finding the solution to being overweight. Of course there is only one solution to being overweight-get off your butt. Inactivity is the greatest cause of obesity. I know very active people who eat me under the table but are thin as a state funded aid society. Why? Because while I watch Baywatch reruns into the wee hours of the morning, burning perhaps two thousand calories a day while taking in three thousand, my cohort is burning off an extra thousand calories by playing tennis, running, building onto his garage and he does this extra activity every day.

The human body was never made to be inactive, except in times of extreme hunger. Our bodies for thousands of years needed to be nimble and quick to out run the very game we needed for our existence, or a surly neighbor at the ready to steal our wives. Human bodies were built to walk, run, jump and throw. Now, when most of us are performing these tasks it is in video games that require about ten calories an hour to play. Hundreds of people have gotten filthy rich by playing on the average person's sympathies. They will show a plump actress in a "before" picture and then show the same actress in an "after" picture next to it. Of course the "after" picture shows a slimmed down, svelte version of the "before" person. This miracle supposedly happened in six weeks using a miracle product called "useless."

Next we are subjected to testimonials either in print or on television each extolling the virtues of the diet and how many other diets they had tried before finding one that really worked. Well I do actually believe the before and after pictures, but the diet that they were on, no matter what the product is called, is known as "starvation" and it always works were others fail because it involves eating no food, which is the very problem in the first place. What I would love to see is an "after, after" picture of the same person two years later. In most cases the person will be fatter than in the "before" picture of years past. Why? Because they starved off about ten pounds of muscle along with the fat and when they returned to their old eating habits their resting metabolism had declined. Some miracle.

I once paid to be on a well-known diet program that cost a reasonable twenty dollars a week for "consultations" but then stuck me for fifty dollars a week for special foods. Most of the food was prepackaged, meaning it had little chance of being on my menu after the diet was over. I did lose weight though, twenty-five pounds. I had to buy new pants and a new belt. My stomach was as flat as a griddle and everyone commented on the new me. I loved it and felt great about the result. About six months later I weighed three pounds more than when I had started the diet and felt more sluggish and depressed than ever before. Now I'm not obese, just not skinny, but still I was furious at myself for having eaten my way back to my original weight plus a few. All that starving, all that money, down the drain. Sound familiar. I'm not alone in this result. Millions of others have suffered the same fate.

Any reasonable person can be made to understand that the secret to losing weight is not dieting, but a diet. A diet is what you eat on a regular and consistent basis that hopefully supplies all of the nutrients and calories one needs to survive. If we all had private chefs with orders to only prepare low fat, healthy foods it would be easy to eat right. Our only concern at that point would be to develop reasonable exercise habits. But most of us do not have a private chef (well Oprah does) so we are faced with the temptation to cook processed and prepackaged foods that are high in calories and low in nutrition. Then of course there are the three-hour nightly stints in front of the television, which require mouth amusement such as chips, popcorn (heavily buttered) and sandwiches. This is where my self and the majority of America get fat. Replace the nightly television with tennis or a long walk and perhaps that miracle you are looking for just might happen.

However, there is another issue in the struggle to be thin. Just what is the optimum weight and how thin is too thin? Calista Flockhart is too thin, way too thin. Most Hollywood actresses are too thin for their own health. Basically we need to be able to touch the floor with our fingertips and have a waistline about ten inches smaller than our chest, if you meet these criteria you are probably all right. We don't need to be a walking skeleton to be attractive. Humans were meant to have a little padding in case of famine. But a little padding and what I see waddling down the sidewalks near a shopping mall are two different things. I see fairly young men and women who are eighty to a hundred pounds overweight shuffling from their car towards the mall entry having just used their handicapped parking sticker to get a spot near the door. Is that absurd or what?

I urge everyone to stop buying useless diet products and start being active. People, there is no other way, but through the taming of your own beast. You and you alone will determine how much you weigh. If it is important enough you will be thin, otherwise I suggest the purchasing of sufficient life insurance now in case you develop diabetes in the future and can no longer obtain it. There is a multitude of worthwhile activities to engage in. Find a few and pursue them, if not, the graveyard waits, and all too soon. There you will be able to lie and stare at the sky all you want. We all have an eternity to sit and watch the world go by, I suggest you use the available time more wisely.

CRITICS

✦

(Or how to make a living without any talent)

Ahhh. Critics. What exactly is a critic, you ask? Well a critic is someone without a shred of creative talent who is paid by a newspaper, a magazine, or a television show to comment on those in society who are blessed to some degree with creative talent. Of course if the critic had any said talent he or she would be pursuing the development of that talent rather than sitting back and envying those that do. Now I am the first to say that some critics serve a purpose. If twenty critics agree that a movie is among the worst they have ever seen then I've probably saved eight bucks on a ticket, but believe it or not even a hundred critics have been wrong before. And what do critics do when the public proves them to have been dead wrong, they perform what I call ratings creep. Watch over a period of time at how a movie that receives "one star" in numerous reviews, but then goes on to make a hundred and fifty million dollars and introduces to the world a star that goes on to make his own millions is listed later on in the local movie guide as a two star or even three star movie. "Bill and Ted's Excellent Adventure" is a perfect example.

Any critic who says they gave the movie a favorable review is lying. It was universally panned. It was labeled a stinker, a farce, and a waste of celluloid. Then an amazing thing happened, people went to the theatre, enjoyed themselves and discovered that a certain star, Keanu Reeves, had a great deal of screen presence, also known as charisma. Suddenly the movie made money, suddenly Keanu was starring in a

195

whole string of hits. What happened to the critics that panned the movie? They disappeared from the earth. I just saw a blurb in the paper for the movie now showing on some backwater cable channel. It was a small paragraph followed by the critics rating of three stars. Three stars! Are you kidding me? That is the very definition of chicken shit. If you thought it was a one star movie then say so, do not revise your opinion after you have been proven to be an idiot, let it out for the whole world to see like the artists whose work you critics love to pan. They don't get a second chance so why should you.

"Ace Ventura Pet Detective" is another example of ratings creep. As most of you know the movie made a couple hundred million dollars and introduced Jim Carey to the world. Now I was very active in movie watching in those days and watched every program on television that rated movies, as well as reading movie magazines and books and newspaper reports, so I well know that no one. NO ONE!!! thought this movie was anything but absolute crap. Roger Ebert curled his chubby nose at the very thought of a talking butt. Well okay, that was a little over the top, but the talent on display in the movie was impossible to ignore. Though I consider myself a cultured and literate person (my god I've actually read <u>War And Peace</u>) I saw the movie twice. I saw genius where the critics saw only talking asses. Perhaps that observation is more a reflection of their personal self-image. I saw "Ace" listed yesterday in the paper, it now has a respectable two stars. The truth is, however, "Ace" is a one star movie. Jim Carey. And I hope that soon he will receive the Academy Award for one of his yet to be released pictures. He would have won it for "The Truman Show" but for the prejudice against him by some critics and voting members for his earlier work. I suggest that the critics climb on his bandwagon or history will one-day record that they could not see genius when it stared them in the face, or talked out its ass.

Writers, too, have their critics. Mostly literary critics are those poor souls that cannot of their selves write a credible story so they take out their unleashed frustrations on those that can. Ernest Hemmingway had his critics. Some thought that his bold masculinity and famous persona had overtaken his good sense and dulled his writing ability. Later in his life he did suffer from creative block, but he also produced The Old Man And The Sea during this period. Unfortunately, not a single person in the critic's circle ever produced a book anywhere near the quality of "The Old Man." Critics do have a way of keeping an artist on his creative toes however, but this is not always healthy. There have been artists, whose nature by definition is sensitive, who have committed suicide after a scathing review by a critic. That, I believe, is giving them far too much credit. Remember that Moby Dick was primarily panned. So why give credence to the words of those who write so poorly they must hack out their pay at a newspaper desk.

Lest I be labeled a critic basher I must report that I have nothing personally against anyone who is working to support a family. But the work of the critic is often absurd. How does one criticize art? Think about it for a moment. Art is the attempt by an artist to interpret the world in a new and beautiful way in order to move the masses from their sofas and into the stream of real life. Don't you find it odd that any one should be criticized for attempting to bring beauty into the world? I do. A singer who uses his or her vocal chords to attempt to bring pleasure to millions should never suffer at the hands of a critic whose work it is to tear down the dreams of artists. On rare occasions a critic actually praises a work that is worthy of praise, but this is usually an accident. Generally it is a third or fourth work by an established artist that receives the critical raves, this after many more intelligent minds have pronounced the man or woman a true artist. I suggest that any new artist that is readily accepted is generally headed for the scrap heap of history. If history has taught us one thing it is that true genius must struggle to capture the imagination of the public, the public is usually out pasturing in another field and must be headed home by the bark of the sublime.

This brings me to my last point. If you are reading this book it is by an accident of nature. If it has been published through conventional means it is a freak of time and space. Hundreds of agents and editors saw a brief excerpt of this book and pronounced it unfit. A few saw potential, but that does not absolve the masses who were too busy staring at their stock portfolio online to even understand what was being presented to them. Thus it is with the world. Critics stand at the gates of paradise and scare off the timid and easily discouraged. I suppose that it is their job. But how many times through the years have the dullards who guard these sacred gates suppressed great art. Too many? I write what I know is true and all the critics in the world will never stop a word of it. I've placed my fate with the public, who have always seen the light of talent basking on the artistic horizon…eventually.

PACKAGING

✤

(Or how do you open these childproof lids?)

ackaging has always been excessive in America. We love to wrap our candy, our foods, and our household supplies in as much wrap as possible. Sometimes the packaging takes up more volume than the product itself, but no amount is deemed too much. We have always been a germ conscious society and rightfully so, but prior to the great Tylenol scam of a few years ago we didn't seal everything on the shelf in impenetrable plastic fortresses. The word child-proof came into play about that time as a way of discouraging rambunctious toddlers from downing one too many Flintstone vitamins, but the result was the absurd notion that child-proof also meant adult-proof. I can attest that on more than one occasion I had to ask my child to open one of these packages for me. How clever this new generation?

Recently I purchased a new bookshelf. I bought it at a nice mall store and assumed because the price I was paying was exorbitant that the product would come fully assembled and ready for display. Wrong! I was told to drive around to the back door and a gentleman would help me load the box into the car. Box? I questioned. I arrived at the back door swinging my back seat door extra wide in order to accept the thirty-inch high bookshelf, but instead a fragile dolly sat wielding a small, flattened box with tight straps. We loaded the box into the car and I was filled with an overwhelming sense of dread. You see, we had recently married and recently moved and we had just spent hours putting together eight or nine new items from basketball hoops to weight benches. I was in no mood for more headaches trying to read indecipherable directions written by people with brilliant technical minds and the writing abilities of advanced chimpanzees.

I sought a solution and it came to me in one of those moments I live for, one of those moments that just screams YES! YES! YES! I would pay my son to assemble it for me. After all, I reasoned, wasn't that what I had fathered children for, to take care of me in my old age? Hadn't the first thing I taught my firstborn been how to change the channels on the television in those days when remote controls were still luxuries. I laid the box on the floor and dangled a ten-dollar bill before my son's eyes. The bookcase was assembled and ready for our living room in a mere half-hour. Simple, he said. I chuckled to myself, my kids always think I'm so dumb, but who was watching HBO while the bookcase magically assembled its self, dumb like a fox. Dad can you clean up the box since I did all this work, my son asked? Certainly, what was the scooping up of a few pieces of cardboard compared to the brain-blistering task of assembling a bookcase, I thought.

I walked down to the basement and there before my eyes laid one of the most god-awful messes I'd ever seen. Cardboard covered half the floor, Styrofoam had spread across the garage floor as if carried on ephemeral wings. I knew I was in trouble. I tried the most reasonable route first, I screamed at my son to get down here and clean up this mess, but he quickly reminded me that I had agreed to clean up and his pay had only included assembling the bookcase. I knew I was cooked and sighed heavily. In all, I counted twenty-three pieces of Styrofoam, or it had been twenty-three pieces originally but by the time I actually captured the last piece it had procreated into more than a hundred tiny pieces. There were in addition twenty pieces of cardboard of various sizes and shapes. It seemed impossible that a bookcase with at best six sections could have generated so much garbage but the evidence lay at my feet in utter disregard for reason. In all I spent an hour and a half cleaning up the mess, or three times longer than my son took to put the bookcase together. A raw deal if ever there was one. I love the bookcase, but I am haunted by the memory of replicating Styrofoam that in my dreams increases to consume the entire world. I have bought nothing with the words "some assembly required" since that day.

I really didn't understand the full impact of packaging in creating waste until my wife finally trained me to start recycling all of the paper that enters our house whether through the mail, the grocery store or work. We used to struggle to fit all of our trash into the receptacle provided, every week stuffing and ramming until the hapless lid could be closed. After recycling paper products, which included anything that was flat, we have never filled the container more than two-thirds full. In short, we generate a lot of paper waste and if you include the newspapers and magazines we read we recycle half of our monthly waste. I understand the need to protect ourselves from loonies, men and woman who would poison us at random, but I think we went a little overboard on the sealed containers. Nowadays even magazines at the bookstore are often shrink-wrapped. What is next, actually having to buy them?

Some day the electronic world will be able to put almost everything we read onto a screen that downloads the printed material we seek without the need for chopping down trees in order to provide the local news. We are a few years off from this, perhaps fifteen years, but it is essential that we learn to read off of a screen or there will not be enough trees left to cut. I look forward to this new world though I hope the screens will have improved and are not so full of glare. We see the first inklings of this trend in e-books and newspaper web sites, but the country as a whole is still miles away from embracing this new technology. How will we take the e-book into the toilet, the public asks? Some day books and magazines will be even more portable than books, perhaps being scrolled across the lenses of a special pair of glasses with a satellite antennae that links us to the entire Library Of Congress, who knows? But I bet when the entire world of knowledge is at our fingertips we will still be struggling to open the package of the aspirin we will so desperately need to squelch our headache from reading too much. And what are reading in this enlightened future age, romance novels of course. We will still need a good cry now and then. In fact, I think I need one now.

HUNGER

◆

(Or how to keep from starving our souls)

There are certain human needs that are readily supplied by the world. The first is oxygen. Though you can buy bottled oxygen for a price it is readily available at no cost just by simply inhaling. No, not all of the air that is free is perfectly clean, but it is enough so that you will be able to sustain life. The next human need is for water. We are primarily made of water and require a good deal of it to survive. This water needs to be free of contamination and disease. With a little effort this is available for most of the world, though there are exceptions. The next need is for sufficient clothing to stay warm enough to sustain life. This seems to be easily obtained for the majority of the world and some people require very little clothing because they live near the equator where it doesn't get cold. This is not to be confused with the need for shelter. The last of our basic biological needs is for enough food to promote growth and to replace the calories burned in working to obtain more food. Food seems to be the most labor-intensive need for most people around the world, though not for Americans.

In America we labor primarily for houses and luxuries to fill them. Food is a relatively minor expense in this country compared to countries around the world. If we were to keep our diet simple (and more nutritious by the way) by eating more unprocessed foods, eating at home more often and by eating more grains and vegetables, rather than expensive cuts of meat, the average American could supply all of his needs for the month in two days of work. Try that in India, it would be more like three weeks. But we rather enjoy the indulgence of a few fineries such as New York steak and eating at Spago's. This is the product of simple economics. You see, we eat the same volume of food regardless of income, so as income rises we simply substitute less desirable products for the more desirable and purchase more service like prepared foods and dining out. This leads to a great absurdity in our society. While millions of Americans are contracting Diabetes and dying young of heart disease, others are starving, or as is more readily the case in America, they are malnourished.

I am going to present an idea which some may deride as heretical. Oh well, I don't mind being burned at the stake. I believe that the four fundamental rights of man are this, and that the government or the people should provide for these rights at large. First is the right to sufficient air to breath, so far so good. Even the most inane government provides this for its people. The second is a little more challenging, but within the realm of reason, all people should be entitled to enough clean drinking water for survival. Third, all people should be given sufficient clothing to provide enough warmth for survival and modesty. No, I am not talking about putting Christian Dior jackets on street kids in Brazil. I am talking about body warmth here, sufficient for survival. My god if we can send people to the top of Mount Everest with sufficient clothing for survival then we can clothe the masses well enough. And fourth, every living person should be given adequate food for survival. No, I don't mean that we should treat Biafrans to a meal at Trader Vic's, I'm talking about survival. That amounts to sufficient calories and nutritional content to sustain life. These rights are fundamental and should be provided to all by their government or by a concerted effort of the people. If a person desires more than this they must earn it, even if they are disabled there are productive avenues for most people. Did you notice that one critical thing was missing from the list? Shelter.

That is my heretical idea, the one for which I will probably be shot. I believe that shelter should be provided by the labor of the individual and should not in any way be the province of the government. If we would concentrate on the first four fundamentals then most people would have sufficient wherewithal to supply the fifth need of shelter. If all of the money spent on government housing (or subsidy payments) had been plowed into the first four principles people would have provided shelter for themselves, and most importantly, taken care of it. Have you ever driven by a housing complex built by the government, especially ten years later. It is all but a cesspool. Why? Because no one has an economic stake in the upkeep. Why? Because at some point they had to divert money to the more fundamental needs of food and clothes. It is a never-ending cycle. But if we place the burden of shelter on the individual while taking care of his fundamental needs he would be better off in the future. Poverty is stress in the extreme, and to know that life will be sustained no matter what relieves the fundamental tension of life in the ghetto. Feed the people, clothe the people and they will do the rest.

Yet it is the decision of nearly every well-meaning government to supply housing to the poor. This is a travesty. The amount of money spent on subsidized housing would literally feed the world. Housing is a societal need and not a fundamental need, just as education is a societal rather than a biological need. I find it strange that we are willing to starve people by giving them half the resources they need for sustenance, while building massive government housing projects that are doomed to failure. Wouldn't we feel better as human beings if instead of 40,000 people starving to death each day the news reports were more like this-40,000 people went without bedrooms today in Pakistan. I think so, and we would be a nobler race for providing for the fundamental needs of our brothers and sisters, for our good fortune comes as much from our good land as anything. Provide the subcontinent of Africa with our natural resources and they too will produce abundance.

Now a secondary byproduct of my proposal would be a decrease in overpopulation. One of the grand designs of the poor in having families of ten children is to ensure that they will be provided for in the future. Remember that social security is not a part of most of the world. (And here I said it was a flawed idea, well only its execution, not its theory.) Freed from the need for food and clothing, having provided shelter for them selves, the poor will not have to rely on the production of children to succeed into old age. This, as you can see, would require a global effort toward food distribution. This could all be accomplished in a generation if people followed the plan. Focus on food and clothing and poverty will cease. We Americans toss out enough food in our garbage to feed a small nation each and every day. If we ate more modestly and distributed more wisely we could and would feed the world. We'd still have finer homes and more luxuries, but that is our natural reward for our productivity and ingenuity. How much better would you sleep at night knowing that no one is hungry because you needed a new car? America gobbles the resources of the world. We owe the world to help solve the problems our consumption causes. We can end hunger in this world. Remember what I said about the middle class, they are invincible. Let us eat cake and have it too.

MANAGEMENT

✦

(Or how to hate your boss while loving the world)

One of my favorite books as a young man was <u>The Peter Principle.</u> I can't tell you how many times I've pondered the ideas in that book during the last twenty years. I believe it is a revelatory book about the nature of American management, but it is flawed in certain respects. The Peter Principle, if you recall, is the proposition that in corporate America managers rise to their level of incompetence. This is not entirely true for Americans are generally appalled by true incompetence. What is truer is that Americans rise to their level of mediocrity. Americans are very forgiving and understanding of the mediocre because most of us fall into that category. The mediocre are left alone to rot out their days in material comfort while the world distances itself from them. Most of us retire in this exact position. Here is why.

When we begin a job we start at the bottom. Having proved a great success at doing the menial labor required at the lower feeding trough we move up to the next trough and begin to feed from there. Some will rise no higher, but a few will master this new level and in time move on up to the next feeding trough were things generally get tough because the next level up is for the precious few. So many careers stall at the third step. What happens is that lower managers successful at supervising workers performing work they themselves understand eventually find themselves in the unenviable task of supervising workers in another area of the business who have more direct knowledge of the work. Here is where the mediocre are doomed to live out their corporate lives. They wallow for years trying to find a way to get people who have greater technical competence to believe in them, enough to be inspired to the heights that propel the manager to the next level. This is the hardest thing on earth to do and only exceptional managers pull it off. I've worked many years in sales and it is a perfect model for the rise of the mediocre because all salesmen are rewarded strictly for their production, which is always viewed by upper management as a sign of greatness to come. Mostly it is a sign that the person should be left alone to sell.

Most of my bosses in sales have had a career very similar to the one I will now describe. First they fail at two or three jobs and find themselves in dire financial straits. Usually they need about twice the income of the average salesman to make ends meet. So they begin to work and put in fourteen-hour days trying to pay the bills and if they have even a modest ability they initially succeed. This is due to the fact that any salesman who sees enough people will ultimately sell enough to earn a living even if they are terrible salesmen. Next the overachiever begins to outshine his cohorts who are only working eight hours a day and he garners the attention of upper management. After that the current sales manager gets promoted because he was smart enough to hire the desperate salesman who is not only making himself rich, but allowing the boss to make a nice bonus as well. Then the inevitable, the top salesman is promoted into the newly created opening and upper management sits back to bask in the glow of the great future of the branch. But something terrible happens. Sales go down, salesmen quit, grumbling under their collars about bastards and horseshit. The primary reason the sales have dropped, however, is that the top salesman just got promoted into management.

So the new manger is told to fire the schlumps and get new blood. So a firing he does go. The new salesmen are bewildered at all of the change, but somehow manage to do about as well as the old group after a month or two. The new manager then realizes that his brilliance as a manager is having little or no effect on sales and that if he wishes to remain a manager he had better do something. So he begins to call numerous sales meetings wherein he threatens the new hires repeatedly with their job and then sits in his office and begins to make sales calls his self, farming the sales out to the schlumps because he is not allowed to get credit for sales. Sales improve and the new manager is transferred where he takes over for a man or woman so incompetent that literally anyone would be an improvement. Sales at the new office improve then level off and the new manager and the upper management reach a state of eternal equilibrium and fifteen years later the new manager, now an old manager, retires. Sound familiar? I've seen it a dozen times at least.

Most people are promoted into management in America for entirely the wrong reasons. It is usually because they did so well at the lower level. Often those with the greatest management potential are those that suck at doing menial labor. So how do these folks get ahead? Some leapfrog the lower level through college, others marry well. I never made it into middle management because sales has the unique structure that often the top salesman makes more than the plant or office manager. I have done it twice. So the correct route for most successful salesmen is to continue selling, yet if you talk to most of the best they will talk vaguely about "getting into management" as if that is a form of retirement for most salesmen. How dead wrong can they possibly be.

Great managers, and I have only worked for two, are those rare individuals who are able to be just successful enough at the lower levels to be considered for promotion. Once they get to the new level that is when their true talents blossom and they make those that work under them feel as if they mattered, which they generally don't. When I've found these true managers I've tried hard to work for them as long as possible though that never works out. They get promoted again, but I do not. In America the greatest managers are hidden in the seams and crevasses of the workplace, making the seemingly competent people above them look good. Most of the managers I've known personally I wouldn't hire to mow my lawn, but then that is often a harder task than running an office where your every decision is made for you from above.

ADVERTISING

✦

(Or how to fleece the public in style)

I was taught in economics 101 that in the early days of manufacturing it was easy to sell a product because there were so few products being sold. Somewhere in the darkness of the twentieth century it became necessary to promote your product so that it got sufficient attention amid the myriad of products available. The world would no longer beat a path to your door if you invented a better mousetrap, I was told. Well, I think that is not true. A better product will always outperform an inferior one. Marketing is a result of equally performing products being sold side by side. The difference in sales over time is in the way equally able products are marketed. I was told in college that marketing is now a science, bullshit, it is and always will be an art.

It is impossible in America to avoid the incessant drone of advertising. It is everywhere, and soon to be in even more places than that. It is on television, on billboards, on posters, in newspapers, on radio. If you haven't seen or heard a particularly memorable ad your friends look at you as if you are depraved or backward. Surely, you had to have seen the one about the shovel and the snowman, they ask incredulously? And the truth is if you haven't seen that particular ad you probably live in a nunnery or a cave. These ads are unavoidable. The advertisers make sure of that.

It is no longer possible to watch a movie on television and not to know the channel on which it is being shown. Tiny icons are emblazoned on the lower right side to assure that the viewer remembers just what channel they are privileged to be watching. Lately, channels have taken to making a small black strip at the bottom of the movie wherein ads appear now and then as intros roll and credits scroll. It is a game of- I'll get you before you can click me. Fun, sort of. But the little icons also get in the way of the picture. We also still click faster than advertisers can paste and cut so they have come up with an entirely new strategy. Putting their ads on things that are shown. Racecars led the way here.

Watch any sporting contest and the ballpark or stadium is filled with advertising. Banners, emblems, displays and hats all fill the eye as the game is being watched. When stats are displayed someone is always presenting them. Coke or Pepsi or god knows whom else. Why are the stats being presented, did those companies compile them? This is a game and the advertisers, I assure you, will always win. There are simply too many ways to compel you to look for advertisers to lose the battle. Even movies, once the province of the trailer, are now being bombarded with ads that air prior to the movie. Home video has had a few ads here and there, but soon you will not be able to rent a movie without ads in the front of the feature presentation. There will be no ad free zones in the future. Toilet paper will one day display ads in pubic places.

The best that one can say about the plethora of ads is that some of them are damn good. Some of the ads are even more entertaining than the shows they support. The Super Bowl is always the groundbreaking for a half dozen new ads that have cost a bloody fortune to produce. Some of the smartest people in America are in advertising. Why? Because that's where the money is, it only used to be in banks. And advertising doesn't stop at the endless purveyance of products. We as a people are not above shameless self-promotion. We are always selling ourselves to customers, prospects, employers and dates. The selling in America doesn't even stop in the bedroom. We are all salesmen whether we like it or not.

And how is everything sold in America-with sex. A dowdy grandma holding a package of Dr. Good's tonic will never do. We must have

Cindy Crawford holding Dr. Good's tonic and saying that her grand-mother used to use it. We hold onto the slimmest inference that we can logically maintain in order to inject a little sex appeal into the matter. And does it work? Like a charm. I have to admit it is much easier to look at Cindy than dear old granny. But there is also a subtler influence that underlies the use of sex, sex appeal, or charisma and that is emotions. If you bought your last car holding a piece of paper in your hand with the suggested purchase price you downloaded off the Internet, and had a price penciled underneath that you were willing to pay, you probably think you are a logical buyer, a person that makes his decisions based solely on the facts and the merits, separated from whimsical emotions. If you believe this I want you take a long look in the mirror and say hello to Mr. Sucker. You are a self-deluded moron. No one. NO ONE!!! Buys anything for logical reasons. We buy to satisfy emotional needs and for no other reason.

I've spent fourteen years of my life successfully selling products and services to nice people. All of them thought they were buying for logical reasons. None of them were. If you buy a new car because you need transportation to work, I would like you to look at all the chrome, the moon roof, the leather seats and the surround sound stereo and explain to me how all of that equipment gets you to work. If you buy a new house because you need shelter explain to me the part your view of Mt. Hood plays in the need to get warm. You see, we are emotional creatures and we buy to satisfy needs we often do not understand. But I understand some of them and so does every other good salesman. And we all know the one secret that propels us to success and you to buy and that is this-every person you will ever meet is exactly one half as smart as they think they are. I've sold security systems to electrical engineers using some of the most twisted logic imaginable. And I did it knowingly just to see how far people would go to justify their purchase. The answer is simple-there is no end. I had a man with a PhD. in engineering agree with me, before I was done with him, that a full moon brings out more criminals and he wanted his system installed pronto so as not to be unprotected by the next lunar cycle. Thank god we weren't too busy as the next full moon was only three days away (he checked.) We got it installed the next day and saved the world for democracy. I was a hero. So what does that make him?

In marketing class they will tell you that advertising needs to be presented so that the fickle public will not forget. But I disagree in part, I believe it is the ads we see, but don't see, that are the most dangerous. These ads have crept into our lives to such an extent that we don't consciously register them. But our subconscious does. I think Coke and Pepsi have done this remarkably well. I've seen many signs a hundred times before realizing there is a Coke symbol attached at the bottom. I believe this explains my incurable habit of drinking three diet Cokes a day. It is not my lack of will, I tell myself, but advertising, always it is the advertising.

No matter how sophisticated or mature we regard ourselves we are still the slaves of the slick sell. Whether that is an ad that prompts us to buy or a salesman who forces money out of our wallets, we are a people doomed to be in debt for all of time because we can. In many ways Americans are the most gullible and easily persuaded people on earth. Why? Because we can afford to make a few mistakes and still feed the kiddies. In other countries buying a vacuum cleaner eighteen times the price of one at the nearest store is simply a recipe for starvation. Americans can afford foolishness so we indulge ourselves. Advertisers and salesman know this all too well and are all too eager to separate you from your money. Except me of course, I buy for purely logical reasons. That is why our family sedan has 270 horsepower.

DRUGS

✦

(Or how high can you fly?)

There was a time when dad would come home from work, pour himself a tall glass of Jack Daniels and drink himself into a blind stupor, those were the good old days. Nowadays it is just as likely that dad smokes a little weed on the side, or even snorts a little cocaine. We have a drug problem in this country that isn't going away any time soon. The root of the problem is our cultural unhappiness that leads us to need alternative realities in the first place. Work is hell we say, I need to unwind. Three gin and tonics later we are most definitely unwound. Drugs are not the sole provinces of the young or even of the unreligious. There is just as much a likelihood of finding a bottle of goodies in Mother Superior's medicine chest as in a teenagers backpack. We all need a little something to get by. Unfortunately, some of us get a little too much medicinal aid and end up dying. Sometimes slowly, as in alcoholism, or instantly as in hurling ourselves out of a fourth story window.

Now I grew up in the sixties and was introduced to drug use in my freshman year of high school. The drugs of choice in that day were of course marijuana, LSD, speed, and downers or reds as they were called. Today we have a plethora of designer drugs that I haven't the time or inclination to recall. Suffice it to say that if one wishes to get high all manner of methods exist. Cocaine came to the fore during the eighties as the drug of choice of the newly rich. By then I was out of that world. I have, like many of my generation, decided to imbibe only legal substances, which are booze and prescription drugs. These are ample means by which to destroy one's self and I deem it wholly unnecessary to break the law.

I was never in doubt as a teenager that a time would come in my life that I'd cease to take illegal drugs. What scares me about young people today is that they don't see drug use as an option, but as a part of life. In other words, they have no desire to ever stop. As science brings us more chemical toys to play with, it may be that a non-drug user in the future may be considered abnormal or plain dumb. However, the human body did not evolve around most of these chemicals and the long-term effects can't always be so easily seen. Remember that people had smoked for two hundred years in this country before anyone knew it caused second hand deaths. So how can we gauge the true risk in mandating a drugged society? We can't. Perhaps the greatest harm comes not to the body but to society that has to deal with the aftermath of the wrecked lives. We as a society are playing with fire and may not only get burned but also incinerated. How can we risk the future over a few snorts of cocaine? I don't know, but we do.

My children inform me that a high percentage of their classmates were first introduced to pot smoking by their parents. Many of my generation still fire up on occasion and think little of it. They then pass along this habit to their offspring who also think nothing of it. So if we are going to smoke pot no matter what, should we legalize it? I don't honestly know. It is a crapshoot either way, but I believe that some form of pot smoking will be allowed in the future and not just for medicinal purposes. Already we have seen countries in Europe so decriminalize the substance as to make it effectively legal for personal use. I do believe that we need to separate pot from more toxic substances such as heroin and morphine. Clearly there is a difference in the outcome of the use of narcotics (a habit which often leads to illegal means of supporting it) and the outcome of weekend pot smoking. The myth that pot smoking leads to harder drugs is just that, a myth. Most of those destined for heroin might use pot for a way station along the trail, but they would get to the heroin with or without pot. Many pot smokers never go forward from there.

And I'm not discussing here parents who work in drudge jobs and smoke weed to forget their troubles. I am talking about professional, otherwise completely responsible, people that I know that smoke pot and make six figures a year. These folks sit on school boards and political action committees, coach little league and lead scout troops. You think not? Get real. Pot smoking is pervasive and impossible at this point to eradicate. So we march on toward an end we cannot see, but I sincerely hope we find a better method in the future to satisfy our needs. We have legalized alcohol, it is so entrenched in all societies as to be permanent. We cannot go back and that is my only fear about marijuana. We can't go back, once legalized it is forever. Even if in some future time we learn that we have inadvertently destroyed the gene pool, we can't go back. So we must proceed with caution. Of course we almost never do.

We have in America a strange relationship with mind-altering substances. We believe in official condemnation with unofficial abuse. Let's take booze for example. In most European countries a child grows up drinking small amounts of wine at the dinner table. By the time that child has reached young adulthood the fascination with getting obliterated out of their minds is gone. They tend to drink in moderation and consider wine and beer to be a condiment rather than a meal. But in America we shield our young from the tyranny of booze until the ripe old age of twenty-one. Never mind that by that age these young people have had sex, used drugs, some even married and a few even fought in battle defending their country. Must keep them from the devil juice, we say. Well that works about as well as my cable company's customer service center. We put onto the alcoholic beverage a status that almost demands its abuse. And if you don't think that the young abuse alcohol I invite you to any college campus near your home on a Saturday night. Some of these students are not drunk, but embalmed.

The deeper question is why? Why do we need to alter our world? Is our daily world all that bad? Yes. Our material culture has robbed us of a spiritual element that once gave purpose to our lives. Material goods cannot love us back, though we can most certainly love them. Inner abundance is a shaky concept in our modern world. It seems to us a waste of time to develop the inner soul while there is so much money to be made. I too have neglected my soul for my wallet on a few occasions, but I was able to pull myself back from the brink. I do drink a few beers and cocktails, but rarely more than one a day. I think I have a good handle on my personal consumption. I drink mostly to unwind, to relax, and this is not a bad thing. Studies have shown that moderate use helps prevent heart disease and may even prolong life. We must never forget that alcohol was invented early on in human society and has been a part of our world for thousands of years. But when we abuse these substances we commit our body to a prison it has difficulty escaping. We were not meant as a species to live in a chemically altered world. We were meant to enjoy the here and now. We used to have to live in the here and now just to survive. I think we still do, we just don't realize it. I hope in the future we alter the outer world to more resemble this inner world we seem compelled to escape into. If not, we may one-day find ourselves leashed to drug therapy from cradle to grave. Were almost there, now that I think about it.

SEXUAL PREFERENCES

✦

(Or how to accept that everyone is the same, yet different)

I was almost ready to end this book with an epilogue that would more or less tie up the loose ends. However, my last section seemed a tad depressing so I decided to include one more statement on our society. And what better way to end things than in a discussion of America's touchiest subject-sex? We are outwardly rather prudish by world standards. We engage in a media feeding frenzy if a public official is caught outside the bonds of marriage. In Europe that would be considered normal or at least understandable. Americans are also intolerant of alternative lifestyles. Here I'm speaking of gays and lesbians cohabitating. Though our laws in most cases protect the rights of these minorities there is clearly an unspoken intolerance of what is deemed by the majority as abnormal behavior.

And just what is abnormal behavior? My neighbors consider it abnormal for a grown man to spend hours each day holed up in his basement typing nonsense onto a computer screen. I consider it abnormal for my neighbors to own houses whose yards have more weeds than grass. In short, abnormal is anything we ourselves do not do on a regular basis. The problem is that everyone is busy doing different things. That is why we rarely talk to our neighbors in this country. They are dissimilar to us. We seek our kind in work and play where we have a more distinct choice in our companions.

In my selling endeavors I've had to go into many thousands of homes all over the Willamette Valley. Thousands. I've seen how people live, actually live and not how they pretend to live when they know company is coming. About half of the time people live within accepted norms of society, but the other half possess at least one abnormality which they ignore, hide, or are just plain too dumb to realize is abnormal. Purple shag carpeting is not normal by my experience, but the lady who owned it thought it the surest sign of good taste. You see, we all interpret normal to mean different things. So although you may appear as Ozzie and Harriet to the outside world that stack of porno tapes in your cabinet makes for remarkable viewing. Though you appear as a roommate to the outside world, the fact that you have one bedroom makes it certain you are a little more. I have often been amused by people's attempts to hide their lifestyles from me. Get a clue folks-I knew.

I can't, after years of entering the homes of gays and lesbians, conclude that their lifestyle is any stranger than say a family of four that spends their weekends at a nudist camp, its weekdays at the PTA. Or how about the artist that hung nude portraits of his wife in the hallway of their home for all to see. Or how about the man whose basement had a padlocked door with a plaque on the wall that read "auditorium." Or how about the woman who's German Shepard appeared a bit more than just a pal. Abnormal? Yep. But we are all abnormal in at least one-way. What is odd to me, because I've seen this oddness first hand, is how society deems a number of abnormal behaviors as illegal and other behaviors as acceptable. We shouldn't judge others until we first judge ourselves. Are we normal? Probably not, at least not entirely.

I'll never forget as long as I live a young man who happened to move into a house nearby when I lived in Lacombe. He moved a few months later so his name escapes me, but he had lived the majority of his life on a dairy where one of his main jobs was to milk cows and feed sheep. One day we were sitting on rails and talking about sex as all fifteen-year-olds will, and I believe at that point the majority of us were still virgins, when we arrived at a discussion of farm animals and this lad blurted out that he had allowed a young sheep to suck on him one day. This was met with contemptible laughter, which caused his face to burn bright red. He said rather sheepishly, (Okay, it is an obvious pun) that all boys did that. At least all the boys he knew. He was truly hoping to hear all of our own stories about the time we let a sheep do the deed on us. But all of us city boys just looked at one another skeptically. We had never even heard of such a thing. I believe that day was the last time most of us ever spoke to the boy. But the thing that always stayed with me was the fact that this young man really believed he was normal. Wholeheartedly. He could not have been more surprised at our response if we had told him we were all eunuchs. So what is normal?

Would you rather live next door to a gay couple or to a pedophile? Would you rather live next door to a cross-dresser or a murderer? Some of us have lived next door to odd people and never known it. Who is it that seems the most shocked when someone is dragged out of their home in handcuffs-it is the neighbors of course? Why, they say, he seemed as normal as you or I. Exactly my point, what is normal? Perhaps we have let our imagination run a little wild when we believe in the grand lie that niceness means acceptable. Hitler used to interrupt high-level German staff meetings to feed ice cream to German school children. What a nice man, the neighbors said.

I think we all get too worked up about our differences. Why do we work so hard against certain behaviors while allowing other, equally absurd behavior? Is it because the Bible tells us so? Maybe. The Bible gives a lot of good advice. Sometimes it is plain outdated. Remember that the target audience for the Bible was primarily nomadic. We wouldn't today consider a man rich because he has a thousand head of sheep. We all know five or six sheep farmers with thousands of head of sheep who all but went bankrupt last year (well okay, those of us that live near sheep farmers did.) So when the Bible gets specific it is often referring only to the immediate audience. It is a bit of a stretch to endow the lessons of the Old Testament onto the modern world. Thou shalt not download MP3 tunes off the Internet for free sayeth the Lord. Check, it is not in there.

So time marches on and society gets more fragmented each day. One day we will all look about and realize that being a little odd IS normal. I'm not normal, I write books, you aren't normal, you wear briefs. But who cares. The things we need to focus on are the true criminal acts. Criminal acts that harm others in a real way, such as robbery, rape, murder and brawls. That should be our focus as a society. Now I do not advocate the compete breakdown of American society. I truly believe that the average person lives his life within certain boundaries even when he is allowed to indulge further. I can drink myself blind every night, in the comfort of my own home, yet I don't. Allowing a behavior does not guarantee its abuse, but for some reason outlawing that same behavior does. It is time to move on as a society. Perfectly sane, nice, functioning adults do many things behind closed doors that are not acceptable. Everyone needs a good spanking now and then. Right?

EPILOGUE

(Or what to title the last section of a book)

I do not presume for you to believe that I've covered the entire gamut of absurdities in American life. I could in reality fill a library with our peccadilloes. In some ways the entirety of American life is absurd, but it does make sense to be as we are, given that we are a free people. Free people make terrible mistakes in electing leaders. Sometimes free people act out of self-interest to the point the majority suffers, but these are minor flaws. For the most part America is a thriving country because of our willingness to embrace our absurdities and yet move forward economically. That takes a great deal of focus don't you think?

Finally, I weeded through many titles for sections to this book. Most were from the cavities of my own cerebral cortex; some sections were suggested (though I'd like to think improved upon) by family and friends. I'd like to list some of these absurdities and let you be the judge of my decision to exclude them. That is bold, I think, to allow the public to decide if one is an idiot or not. Here goes. Strip malls sitting half empty, the right to die, vacations, caller ID, whims of fashion, Braille on ATM's at drive-up windows, vegetarianism, insurance rip-offs, furniture stores that constantly go out of business, golf courses in deserts, the over breeding of dogs and cats, colleges purchasing 250,000 dollar billboards to market a player for the Heisman Trophy, spoiled kids whose parents try to buy their love, pet deposits (at apartments, not on the carpet I presume), errors on credit reports, and last but not least, the absurdity of writing a book on absurdity. So I think you can plainly see that it was a damn good thing that I did what I did.

So I conclude with this warning. Do not give this book to your neighbor to read. This is officially a reference book. You will need to refer back to it from time to time as the mood demands. So tell your neighbor to get his own copy and please be sure to pay for it-do not, I repeat DO NOT steal this book. I'm not Abbie Hoffman. I have a mortgage. I hope you have enjoyed our brief run through America. I'm winded, how about you? Lastly, I'd like to thank the people of America throughout the decades who have contributed to this book by their odd behavior, without them a book on absurdity would not have been possible. But in truth, America itself would not have been possible. America is a concept that has evolved by constant human experiment. If we ever do remove absurdity from our lives, we will all have been cloned. I'll take my chances on fate.

About the Author

Allen L. Scarbrough lives in Tigard, Oregon and is the father of four children. He is the author of three books and one screenplay.

0-595-22068-1